GROWING UP IN IOWA

GROWING UP IN IOWA

REMINISCENCES OF 14 IOWA AUTHORS

EDITED BY
CLARENCE A. ANDREWS

IOWA STATE UNIVERSITY PRESS / AMES

CLARENCE A. ANDREWS is author of many books and articles in regional literature and history. He holds the Ph.D. in English from the University of Iowa and is presently visiting professor of journalism and adjunct professor of English there.

ACKNOWLEDGMENTS

Hamlin Garland, "Going for the Doctor," in *A Son of the Middle Border,* Macmillan, New York, 1917, pp. 139–43. Copyright © renewed 1945 by Mary I. Lord and Constance G. Williams. Reprinted with permission of Macmillan.

Frank Luther Mott, "The Old Printing Office," in the *Palimpsest,* Jan. 1962 (copyright © 1962 by State Historical Society of Iowa), and in *Time Enough,* 1962 (copyright © 1962 by University of North Carolina Press, Chapel Hill). Reprinted by permission of the publishers.

James Stevens, "Medicine Men: Reminiscences," in the *American Mercury,* 28 Apr. 1933, pp. 487–97. Reprinted by permission of *American Mercury,* Torrance, Calif.

Richard Harsh, drawing for "Medicine Men: Reminiscences," from charcoal drawings of Moravia, Iowa, town square, prepared for 125th anniversary of Moravia in 1976.

Phil Stong, "Matriculation," in *If School Keeps,* Matson, New York, 1940. Reprinted by permission.

Paul Engle, "Newsboy's Christmas," in *An Old Fashioned Christmas,* Dial Press, New York, 1964. Copyright © 1964 by Paul Engle. Reprinted by permission of the author.

Frederick Manfred, "Winter Count," in *Winter Count,* Brown, New York, 1966. Copyright © 1966 by Frederick Manfred. Reprinted by permission of Curtis Brown, Ltd., New York.

Richard Bissell, "Not a Difficult Feat, Even for a Boy," from *My Life on the Mississippi, or Why I Am Not Mark Twain.* Copyright © by Richard Bissell, by permission of Little, Brown and Co., Boston, 1973, pp. 32–33, 37–41 (edited).

Paul Corey, "The Hunt," in *The Road Returns,* Bobbs-Merrill, Indianapolis, 1940, pp. 380–91. Copyright © 1940 by Paul Corey. Reprinted by permission of the author.

Composed and printed by
The Iowa State University Press
Ames, Iowa 50010

First edition, 1978
Second printing, 1978

Library of Congress Cataloging in Publication Data
Main entry under title:

Growing up in Iowa.

    1. Iowa—History, Local—Addresses, essays, lectures. 2. Iowa—Biography—Addresses, essays, lectures. I. Andrews, Clarence A.
F621.5.G76   977.7   78-2375
ISBN 0-8138-1940-7

CONTENTS

Introduction   vii

HAMLIN GARLAND
  Going for the Doctor   3

FRANK LUTHER MOTT
  The Old Printing Office   9

JAMES STEVENS
  Medicine Men: Reminiscences   17

PHIL STONG
  Matriculation   33

JAMES HEARST
  Young Poet on the Land   39

PAUL ENGLE
  Newsboy's Christmas   61

FREDERICK MANFRED
  Winter Count   67

RICHARD BISSELL
  Not a Difficult Feat, Even for a Boy   81

PAUL COREY
  The Hunt   89

CLARENCE ANDREWS
  Did You Ever See a Dream Walking—?   101

JULIE McDONALD
  Growing Up in Western Iowa   113

RICHARD LLOYD-JONES
    Fire and Ice: A Rhapsodic View of the 30s   125

ROBERT BOSTON
    Spring, 1955   133

WINIFRED MAYNE VAN ETTEN
    Three Worlds   141

INTRODUCTION

AS PAUL ENGLE has somewhere intimated, Iowa, the "beautiful land," is a place of both pigs and poets. Now pigs abound in Iowa; touring through the state, day or night, one can hardly be unaware of their presence. Together with the corn on which they fatten, they give the state its reputation for being bountiful as well as beautiful. Yea, as we saw in Phil Stong's *State Fair,* there are those who see beauty in a well-fed porcine profile.

But your average Iowan, like all humankind, is not only a materialistic creature. Hungry or satiated, the search continues for meaning in existence, romance in life, feeling in everyday happenings. The Iowa author, poet or novelist, helps him or her find romance, focus on experience, understand its meaning, sharpen perceptions, *feel* the way along. Sometimes it does seem that the author *is* one with a deeper understanding or a better handle on the language. Sometimes, perhaps, it's just a case of the author having more time to think about these matters because the hog- (and corn-) raiser is willing to share some hard-gotten gains with others. Genius expresses itself in both the hog lot and the study, but the person slaving *in* the pen has little time or energy left *for* the pen!

Whatever the case, on the following pages you will find well-chosen words about what it means to grow up in Iowa by people who could take time to think about their past, and you will discover that at least one of these Iowans took time off from swilling the pigs to do his thinking! They are all Iowans, these authors—they all grew up in Iowa and quite a few of them have spent most of their lives there. They know the clear distinction between a silk purse and a sow's ear, even though some of them may never have possessed either.

Three are poets, although all three have occasionally turned their hand to prose. One of the poets and all but one of the rest are novelists, although one of the novelists is here represented in verse. The fourteenth is a writer of nonfiction.

The selection of materials covers most regions of the state and most of the years since about 1860, the period that Hamlin Garland first wrote about in his *Boy Life on the Prairie.* Garland's offering describes a wild night ride across the open northeast Iowa prairie for the doctor in the distant town. Then Frank Luther Mott tells us about a small-town printing plant in the 1890s, one of the beginnings of industry and communications in the state. The period from 1900 to 1920 is covered by descriptions of central Iowa farm life (James Hearst), small-town life in a southern Iowa coal-mining community (James Stevens), first school days in a small southeast Iowa town (Phil Stong), a Frisian community in the far northwest corner of the state (Frederick Manfred), a newsboy's Christmas in Cedar Rapids (Paul Engle), a wolf hunt in far southwest Iowa (Paul Corey), life on the

Mississippi (Richard Bissell), and a boy's adventures at the movies in an eastern Iowa city (Clarence Andrews).

Julie McDonald describes farm and small-town life in a western Iowa Danish settlement a few years later, and Richard Lloyd-Jones reminisces about childhood and boyhood in the 1930s in north central "River City." A much younger Iowa author, Robert Boone, talks about a spring moment in central Iowa in 1955.

Finally, Winifred Mayne Van Etten looks back over her lifetime in Iowa from before World War I through both of our major twentieth century wars to the present.

It's not by any means the whole picture. I would have liked to include some of Leonard Brown's pioneer poem about Iowa when native Americans were still everywhere, some of MacKinlay Kantor's autobiography from *Look the Morn,* some of "Steamboat Bill" Petersen's memoirs, or part of Ruth Suckow's *Some Others and Myself.* I'd like to have seen something by Thomas Duncan here. That goes for Curt Harnack and Marjorie Holmes also, but at least their reminiscences of growing up in Iowa are current. I could name many other Iowa authors. Some, of course, have gone to that great publishing house in the sky and left no memoirs behind. Others, for one reason or another, including space limitations and the patience of a reading public, are not here. If you don't find a favorite author here, please be assured it has nothing to do with the likes or dislikes of the editor. As I have made perfectly clear elsewhere, I am a wholehearted advocate of Iowa authors and the literature they have produced.

Perhaps this "Whitman's Sampler" of Iowa authors will persuade you to head for your favorite bookstore or library to see what else Iowans have written. And if you're hungry, literally as well as figuratively, you'll discover there are few combinations more rewarding than an Iowa novel, an Iowa ham sandwich, and a cold glass of Iowa milk!

GROWING UP IN IOWA

Hamlin Garland

THE INCIDENT related in "Going for the Doctor," a tale of a nighttime emergency on the open prairie, took place about 1875. The Garlands at that time lived north and east of Osage, Iowa, in Mitchell County, on a farm still identified today as the Garland farm. The run out to the farm today in a comfortable car over good all-weather roads seems very short, but it must have seemed an eternity to the boy Hamlin.

It is not easy to trace Hamlin's ride on 1875 maps. No diagonal road shows on maps of the time. But William Biederman of Osage says that the road did indeed run northeast out of town, although it does not exist today.

Osage was platted by a Dr. S. B. Chase and some associates. Four doctors were in Osage at the time this incident took place, but it is quite likely that Chase was the man selected. The Clay-Banks team would certainly indicate some affluence.

Chase's home, office, and servants' quarters were in a long building that still stands in Osage today. Dr. Chase lived in the east wing of this building, his office was in the center wing, and the servants' quarters were in the west wing.

Hamlin Garland was born at West Salem, Wisconsin, in 1860. In 1869, his father brought the family to Winneshiek County near the Minnesota line, and then, within a year or so, to Osage, where Garland was educated. He was author of poems, short stories, novels, autobiographical books, and one play. His *Middle Border* books are still a delight to read with their accounts of life on the prairie as it was being converted to farmland. He is the most significant author among Iowa writers, a major influence on the kind of literary realism that has dominated American literature in this century. His *A Daughter of the Middle Border* (1921) won the Pulitzer Prize for autobiography, although the award obviously should have been made to *A Son of the Middle Border* (1917) from which this selection was taken. He died in 1940, widely acknowledged as the "dean of American letters."

GOING FOR THE DOCTOR

ONE NIGHT as I lay buried in deep sleep close to the garret eaves I heard my mother call me—and something in her voice pierced me, roused me. A poignant note of alarm was in it.

"Hamlin," she called, "get up—at once. You must go for the doctor. Your father is very sick. *Hurry!*"

I sprang from my bed, dizzy with sleep, yet understanding her appeal. "I hear you, I'm coming," I called down to her as I started to dress.

"Call Hattie. I need her too."

The rain was pattering on the roof, and as I dressed I had a disturbing vision of the long cold ride which lay before me. I hoped the case was not so bad as mother thought. With limbs still numb and weak I stumbled down the stairs to the sitting room where a faint light shone.

Mother met me with white, strained face. "Your father is suffering terribly. Go for the doctor at once."

I could hear the sufferer groan even as I moved about the kitchen, putting on my coat and lighting the lantern. It was about one o'clock of the morning, and the wind was cold as I picked my way through the mud to the barn. The thought of the long miles to town made me shiver but as the son of a soldier I could not falter in my duty.

In their warm stalls the horses were resting in dreamful doze. Dan and Dick, the big plow team, stood near the door. Jule and Dolly came next. Wild Frank, a fleet but treacherous Morgan, stood fifth and for a moment I considered taking him. He was strong and of wonderful staying powers but so savage and unreliable that I dared not risk an accident. I passed on to bay Kittie whose bright eyes seemed to inquire, "What is the matter?"

Flinging the blanket over her and smoothing it carefully, I tossed the light saddle to her back and cinched it tight, so tight that she grunted. "I can't take any chances of a spill," I explained to her, and she accepted the bit willingly. She was always ready for action and fully dependable.

Blowing out my lantern I hung it on a peg, led Kit from her stall out into the night, and swung to the saddle. She made off with a spattering rush through the yard, out into the road. It was dark as pitch but I was fully awake now. The dash of the rain in my face had cleared my brain but

I trusted to the keener senses of the mare to find the road which showed only in the strips of water which filled the wagon tracks.

We made way slowly for a few minutes until my eyes expanded to take in the faint lines of light along the lane. The road at last became a river of ink running between faint gray banks of sward, and my heart rose in confidence. I took on dignity. I was a courier riding through the night to save a city, a messenger on whose courage and skill thousands of lives depended.

"Get out o' this!" I shouted to Kit, and she leaped away like a wolf, at a tearing gallop.

She knew her rider. We had herded the cattle many days on the prairie, and in races with the wild colts I had tested her speed. Snorting with vigor at every leap she seemed to say, "My heart is brave, my limbs are strong. Call on me."

Out of the darkness John Martin's Carlo barked. A half-mile had passed. Old Marsh's fox hound clamored next. Two miles were gone. From here the road ran diagonally across the prairie, a velvet-black band on the dim sod. The ground was firmer but there were swales full of water. Through these Kittie dashed with unhesitating confidence, the water flying from her drumming hooves. Once she went to her knees and almost unseated me, but I regained my saddle and shouted, "Go on, Kit."

The fourth mile was in the mud, but the fifth brought us to the village turnpike and the mare was as glad of it as I. Her breath was labored now. She snorted no more in exultation and confident strength. She began to wonder—to doubt, and I, who knew her ways as well as I knew those of a human being, realized that she was beginning to flag. The mud had begun to tell on her.

It hurt me to urge her on, but the memory of my mother's agonized face and the sound of my father's groan of pain steeled my heart. I set lash to her side and so kept her to her highest speed.

At last a gleam of light! Someone in the village was awake. I passed another lighted window. Then the green and red lamps of the drug store cheered me with their promise of aid, for the doctor lived next door. There too a dim ray shone.

Slipping from my weary horse I tied her to the rail and hurried up the walk toward the doctor's bell. I remembered just where the knob rested. Twice I pulled sharply, strongly, putting into it some part of the anxiety and impatience I felt. I could hear its imperative jingle as it died away in the silent house.

At last the door opened and the doctor, a big blonde handsome man in a long night gown, confronted me with impassive face. "What is it, my boy?" he asked kindly.

As I told him he looked down at my water-soaked form and wild-eyed countenance with gentle patience. Then he peered out over my head into

". . . I lay buried in deep sleep
close to the garret eaves . . ."

HAMLIN GARLAND BIRTHPLACE, BUILT BY HIS FATHER IN 1869, 3½ MILES NORTH OF OSAGE.

"I could hear its imperative jingle as it died away in the silent house."

the dismal night. He was a man of resolution but he hesitated for a moment. "Your father is suffering sharply, is he?"

"Yes, sir. I could hear him groan.—Please hurry."

He mused a moment. "He is a soldier. He would not complain of a little thing—I will come."

Turning in relief, I ran down the walk and climbed upon my shivering mare. She wheeled sharply, eager to be off on her homeward way. Her spirit was not broken, but she was content to take a slower pace. She seemed to know that our errand was accomplished and that the warm shelter of the stall was to be her reward.

Holding her down to a slow trot I turned often to see if I could detect the lights of the doctor's buggy which was a familiar sight on our road. I had heard that he kept one of his teams harnessed ready for calls like this, and I confidently expected him to overtake me. "It's a terrible night to go out, but he said he would come," I repeated as I rode.

At last the lights of a carriage, crazily rocking, came into view and pulling Kit to a walk I twisted in my saddle, ready to shout with admiration of the speed of his team. "He's driving the 'Clay-Banks,' " I called in great excitement.

The Clay-Banks were famous throughout the county as the doctor's swiftest and wildest team, a span of bronchos whose savage spirits no journey could entirely subdue, a team he did not spare, a team that scorned petting and pity, bony, sinewy, big-headed. They never walked and had little care of mud or snow.

They came rushing now with splashing feet and foaming, half-open jaws, the big doctor, calm, iron-handed, masterful, sitting in the swaying top of his light buggy, his feet against the dash board, keeping his furious span in hand as easily as if they were a pair of Shetland ponies. The nigh horse was running, the off horse pacing, and the splatter of their feet, the slash of the wheels and the roaring of their heavy breathing, made my boyish heart leap. I could hardly repress a yell of delight.

As I drew aside to let him pass the doctor called out with mellow cheer, ''Take your time, boy, take your time!''

Before I could even think of an answer, he was gone and I was alone with Kit and the night.

My anxiety vanished with him. I had done all that could humanly be done, I had fetched the doctor. Whatever happened I was guiltless. I knew also that in a few minutes a sweet relief would come to my tortured mother, and with full faith and loving confidence in the man of science, I jogged along homeward, wet to the bone but triumphant.

''The Clay-Banks were famous
throughout the county as the doctor's
swiftest and wildest team . . .''

''CLAY-BANKS'' REFERS TO THE COLOR OF THE TEAM DRIVEN BY THE DOCTOR IN THIS STORY.

State Historical Society of Iowa collection

❦ ❦ Frank Luther Mott

FRANK LUTHER MOTT is also a Pulitzer Prize winner, his award coming in 1939 for his four-volume *A History of the American Magazine*. He is author of several other books, including an autobiography, *Time Enough* (1962), and numerous shorter pieces. He was editor and publisher of two important periodicals, the *Midland,* with John Towner Frederick, and the *Journalism Quarterly.*.

William J. Petersen calls Mott one of Iowa's most distinguished native sons. He was born on a Keokuk County farm, and with his itinerant Quaker newspaper-publisher father and mother he lived in What Cheer, Tipton, Audubon, and Marengo. Mott's father wanted him to become a newspaper man also, but Mott turned to teaching during World War I (after serving as editor and publisher of the *Grand Junction Globe*). For twenty-one years he was closely associated with the University of Iowa, serving ultimately as director of the School of Journalism. Later he became dean of the School of Journalism of the University of Missouri.

"The Old Printing Office" is excerpted both from a *Palimpsest* article of 1962 and *Time Enough*. In the same issue of the *Palimpsest* (and in the book) is a longer essay, "Country Town," well worth the reading.

What Cheer, Iowa, in the 1890s was a town of 3246 people who were largely engaged in coal mining. Tipton was half the size but growing whereas What Cheer was losing population. No doubt for a Quaker family Tipton was a more pleasant place to live than a rough-and-tumble coal mining town. Mott's father needed only two men and a woman to help him with the *What Cheer Patriot,* but his *Tipton Advertiser* "force" consisted of two men and two women.

Weekly newspaper publishing was largely a barter economy in those days. The local post office was required by law to deliver the weekly within the county free of charge. Farmers often paid for their subscriptions with produce. The "patent insides" of which Mott speaks paid for the paper on which the newspaper was printed. At a dollar or so for a year's subscription, there was very little cash to pay the force.

The first part of the week was spent in soliciting advertisements and laying them out, gathering news items ("Mr. and Mrs. Thomas Jones and children had Sunday dinner at the home of the gentleman's parents"), setting them in type, and preparing for the Thursday evening "run." If it was mild weather and the ink rolls didn't melt and if the press didn't act up, all went well—provided the male members of the force could stay sober. Any job printing ʰhat fell to the lot of the newspaper was done on Fridays and Saturdays.

Small wonder that the Motts were an itinerant family, always looking for greener pastures elsewhere.

THE OLD PRINTING SHOP

WE CALLED IT a "country" printing office, because its chief output was a "country" newspaper. Nowadays we talk of the "community" newspaper. The word "country" is now applied mainly to hillbilly music and a curious kind of fellow known as a "bumpkin" or a "hayseed." Like the words "villain," "boor," and "churl," all of which originally meant countryman or farmer, the word "country" itself seems to have descended in the scale of respectability. The philological standing of this word-symbol appears to have followed the downward curve of the countryman's economic status.

My father was not ashamed to call himself a "country" editor: he was proud of the designation and the vocation. He hoped I might follow in his footsteps; and in recommending such a career to me when I was a boy, he said that it had been his observation that, except for an occasional rascal or drunkard, the editor was always looked up to in his small community. It might not be a big puddle, Father said, but the editor was always one of the big frogs in it. I think that was true. Whatever hierarchy of leadership the country town possessed held assured places for the editors—or at least one of the editors of the two or three local papers. The editor was usually a political oracle; and he was sometimes sent to the legislature or appointed to state office. He was actually a liaison bringing the outside world of events and situations together with the life of the home community. He was supposed to be the best informed man in town on questions of the day. "They expect the editor to know everything," said my father, and added, "You must get a good college education."

The plant from which he issued his weekly newspaper and in which he conducted a job-printing business consisted of a "front office" and a "back office." The former was much the smaller and was devoted to editorial and management activities, and the latter contained the mechanical department. In most Midwestern towns in the Eighteen-nineties, the printing office was all in one room; and that was chiefly because the editor and manager was himself a printer and carried his editorial sanctum with him while he worked at the case or the press. Entering the front door of such an office, one walked directly into a

"My father called his group of employees 'the force.'"

fascinating confusion of characteristic smells, sounds, litter, and orderliness within disorder. But in our shops there was always a "front office," because Father had never learned the printer's trade; and besides he liked privacy for conferences with visitors, for business transactions, and for writing.

I set my first type in the office of my father's Tipton *Advertiser* in 1896, when I was ten years old. My first copy was a piece of reprint credited to "Ex." to indicate that it had been taken from some paper obtained by "exchange"; and it probably had bounced around among many papers before Father had clipped it from one of his own "exchanges." It was a bit of verse with "run-in" instead of broken lines, dealing with a man's troubles in the Spring, from house-cleaning, wet feet and colds, too much gardening, and so on, in which every stanza (paragraph) ended with the plaintive plea: "Listen to my tale of wo!" It took me three or four evenings, working after school, to get this masterpiece of wit into pica type. I had almost finished the second stickful when, in my awkwardness, I dropped the whole thing on the floor. The printers laughed, thinking that now the boy was getting his first experience with pi; but when I scrambled down off the high stool to pick up the remains, I found the type intact in the stick! I had not learned to justify my lines properly, but had forced thin spaces in so that every line was very tight; indeed they were so tight that the type could scarcely be removed from the stick when it was ready for dumping on the galley.

I had plenty of experience with pi after that, however. Some years later, helping out in a rush hour when we were late getting to press, I removed my case, which was "poor" in type by that time, from the stand in order to shake it (a method of getting the remaining type out of the corners of the boxes and making it easier to pick up); but in my clumsy hurry, I dropped the entire case. There it was, pied all over the floor. I turned in dismay toward the foreman—and knocked a full galley of type ready for the forms off a galley rack. If I had not been the editor's son, I should have been booted out of the back door.

But usually setting type was, if not fun, at least mildly pleasurable. Monotonous it was, indeed, but there were always the twin challenges of speed and accuracy. On a Saturday, when cases were full and the office was clean and comparatively quiet after the hurly-burly of a Thursday press-day, followed by the "throwing-in" of Friday, when the type was returned to the cases—then it was that setting type was peculiarly satisfying. Beginning with a new case, the boxes rounded up full, and the type cool and damp from fresh distribution, was a little like sitting down before a generously loaded table—just as working from an almost empty case, with dust at the bottom of the boxes, had been like starvation diet.

Sometimes the copy itself was interesting and instructive. I enjoyed setting up my father's editorial in bourgeois (pronounced berjoice); and I was always pleased when I found an excerpt from the current *McClure's* or *Harper's,* sent out by the magazine as promotion, on my hook. But how inexpressibly boresome was the monthly job of setting the patent medicine notices in nonpareil!

My father called his group of employees "the force." It consisted of a foreman, two all-'round printers, two lady compositors, and a "devil" who worked after school and on Saturdays.

At least, such was the personnel when my brother and I took turns "deviling" on the Tipton *Advertiser* in the Mid-Nineties. Our duties ranged from sweeping the floor and burning trash in the back yard to setting type and learning to feed the small jobber. Cleaning up after press-day was no easy task, for wastepaper, rags grimy with grease from the press, and dabs of sticky printer's ink seemed to be everywhere. Moreover, our job was complicated by the printers' habit of chewing tobacco. It was commonly said that printers were subject to lead-poisoning because they were constantly handling type, which contains a considerable proportion of lead in its composition, and that the best antidote was chewing tocacco. This was probably a medical fable invented as an alibi by nicotine users; however, most printers chewed plug-tobacco, and the "devil" had to cope with their expectoration. We improvised spittoons from the heavy, small boxes in which we had received shipments of type and plates, filling them with sawdust and placing them conveniently near the type-stands, stones, and presses; but the chewer's aim was often imperfect.

Father was always particular about his foremen, and I remember them all as men of good character and some skill in "the art perservative of arts." Three papers that Father owned at various times he eventually sold to his foremen. For the other printers he often had to take what he could get, and they sometimes drank too much; indeed, I remember that we were often late with the first issues following the Fourth of July and Christmas because of trouble getting reorganized after the sprees that many printers regarded as their right on those holidays. I do not wish to wrong the average printer of those days: many of them were men of industrious habit and excellent character. My Uncle Artie worked in Father's printing office for several years; he was a fine, spruce young man who excited my unbounded admiration by dressing up in approved bicycle costume—sweater, tight pants, and black stockings—in the evenings and riding a highwheeler along the wooden sidewalks and dusty streets of What Cheer.

Itinerant printers appeared once in a while, and sometimes, when job-work was plentiful, they were welcomed and put immediately to work. They came unannounced from nowhere, and they disappeared without warning into limbo. They had rainbows 'round their shoulders that lured them always to the next town, or into the next state. "Tourist typos" my father called them. They usually brought some curious craft secrets with them—a new ingredient for our home-made blocking glue, a secret for a paste for "single wraps," a formula for an ink to imitate embossing.

Usually these wanderers would stay with us no more than three or four weeks at the most, but I remember one man in his thirties who declared his intention to settle down, and who stuck with us for over a year. He was the son of parents who were circus performers and he had been trained as a child aerialist; but a fall from a trapeze had injured his feet and turned him from the big tops to the printing office. He was tattooed all over the upper part of his body; and when he worked near the big window of the shop in the summertime with his shirt off for coolness, he drew such a crowd on the sidewalk and made such a scandal that a sleeveless undershirt had to be prescribed as minimum clothing. Whether this offended him, or what it was, one morning he simply did not show up. He left no debts behind him; indeed he had a couple of days' pay due him and he had paid his landlady ahead for board and room. Apparently the old wanderlust had carried him off between days. We never heard of him again.

The climax of the week in the printing office was the Thursday press-day. The stress and strain, hustle and hurry of the weekly effort to "get out" on time brought the whole office to a high pitch of activity. Putting the last paragraphs of news in type picked from nearly empty cases, setting the last heads, correcting the galley proofs with swift care, marking and placing the corrected galleys for the make-up man—all these things were parts of the planned urgency of press-day. What a welcome sound was the rat-tat-tat of mallet on planer which announced that the front-page form was ready to lock up in its chase! While the heavy form was being transferred to the bed of the press, we were laying clean papers on the stones and tables in readiness for the operation of hand-folding the edition. Also someone was preparing the patent mailer which, when it worked, addressed the folded papers; and another was laying out the wrappers for the single-list of papers to be dispatched to a distance. To help with the folding, the editor often recruited his whole family. My own mother, when her family was small, used to help fold papers on press-day. Some editors' wives worked so much in the office that they became practical printers, and occasionally one of these small plants was operated entirely by the editor's family. But on any paper, the tensions of press-day were bound to affect all the editor's family, and everyone helped as he or she could—with the news, the mechanical work, the folding, wrapping, and mailing, and the final carting of the papers to the post office.

My father was a controversialist in his editorial columns, especially on party matters; but he was never violent. . . . Occasionally [he] would with some effort strike a lighter note. The most famous piece he ever wrote was about a prayer he had heard a country preacher offer one Sunday. This was in the midst of the drought of 1898, and also in the time of the Spanish-

"He was a fine, spruce young man . . ."

MOTT'S UNCLE ARTIE AT THE TYPE CASE, WHAT CHEER, CIRCA 1890.

American War. Here is the prayer as Father set it down on his arrival at home, and as he published it in his paper the following week:

> . . . And O Lord, we ask for rain. Thou has taught us to come to Thee to ask for what we need; and we need rain. Thy servants of old prayed for rain, and their prayers were heard. Elijah prayed for rain, and his prayer was answered. The ground is parched, the grass is dying, the heat oppresses us so we can hardly breathe. O Lord, give us refreshing rain!
>
> We prayed for rain last week, and it has not come yet. Perhaps we did not need it as badly as we thought. Now the farmers say we will not have half a crop unless we have rain soon, but then some would say that anyway. But we know we need rain! O Lord, we need money to carry on this righteous war for humanity, and we need crops to get the money with; so, Lord, give us rain that we may have the crops.
>
> Thou hast tempered the winds to our battleships. The typhoons and the hurricanes of the Tropics have not molested them. Thou hast given us the victory, and we praise Thy name. . . .

The story ended simply by telling how, as the editor drove home that afternoon, he noticed a cloud in the Northwest "as small as a man's hand," and how that night the whole countryside received a generous downpour.

My father never thought his work trivial or of little consequence. We all looked upon our paper as the historian of many lives. We know that we put the town and country down in black and white—joys and sorrows, good and ill, peace and war, prosperity and failure. We watched the growth and development of the community, the decay of some institutions, the setting of new patterns. Our paper recorded all these things, bringing our people and the little episodes of their lives and the town's events together within the compass of a few columns weekly. Thus any country paper welds together all the elements of its social group in a continuing history.

The country paper of the Nineties and the first decade of the new century seems to me to have performed three services—in some instances badly, indeed, but in many very well. It was the contemporary historian of local events; it offered an editorial column that was often thoughtful and sometimes influential; it contributed to the economic welfare of its community by affording an advertising medium and by acting as a leader in progressive movements.

For many years now, everything in America has been irresistibly swept up into the prodigious heaps of the great cities and their sprawling suburbs. But home-town papers remain to serve many small towns throughout the nation. The weekly of today, however, is not the same country paper I knew as a boy; it has a linotype, it is illustrated by local pictures, it is smarter, it serves its advertisers better. Nor is the town it serves the same; it is no longer a semi-isolated hamlet, undisturbed by the blare of automobile horns, unstirred by the incursion into its midst of the strange phantasmagoria of ''show business'' on electronic screens in every home.

But in spite of changing patterns, the home paper of today has the same spirit of neighborliness and service that it has always had, and continues to integrate the life of its community.

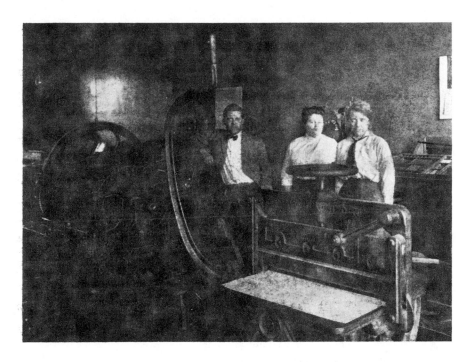

''But home-town papers remain
to serve many small towns
throughout the nation.''

FRANK LUTHER MOTT AND HIS PRINTSHOP STAFF.
GRAND JUNCTION, CIRCA 1914.

𝕮 𝕮 James Stevens

NOT ALL OF Iowa was farmland and many Iowans made their living at occupations other than farming. In Frank Luther Mott's What Cheer and elsewhere, men made their living digging into the seams of soft coal they found just under the sod, as outcroppings along creek bluffs, and at greater depths. This was particularly true in Van Buren, Wapello, Monroe, Appanoose, Keokuk, Wayne, Lucas, and Mahaska counties, and in the broad Des Moines River valley up through Polk, Boone, and Webster counties. Many a small village or "location" grew up around the strip mines and the slag heaps of the "doghole" mines.

Among the towns in these counties that were the center of both farming and coal-mining activities was Moravia, in southern Iowa, halfway between Albia, county seat of Monroe County, and Centerville, county seat of Appanoose County, both major coal-producing areas. Moravia, as Stevens's story implies, was named for a religious sect that settled in the area.

But, as "Medicine Men" (1933) indicates, more than just farmers and coal miners lived in this raw prairie town. Every town had its Tunk Chambers and its Pleas Repp, whose ways of life contrasted with the more pious, sedate lives of the solid citizens. Not every town had its patent medicine factory, but there were a great many of these. In the Upper Peninsula of Michigan, a French-speaking priest from Belgium for a time concocted a vile-tasting panacea from herbs whose seeds he had brought with him and managed to sell a few thousand bottles. As Stevens's story implies, the major ingedient in such fluids was either a strong portion of alcohol or a pain-numbing drug such as opium. They didn't cure but they brought relief.

In another of Stevens's stories about Moravia, we learn that the area was inhabited by Hard-Shell Baptists (among them his grandmother), horse traders, "idolatrous Papists," and Methodists, producing an environment that reduced hatred of original sin to a prohibition against loitering around the local livery stable. The Indian, such as John Badax, was a less common feature—this one was undoubtedly imported by Bearpaw.

Blacks, however, were fairly common in southern Iowa towns. One coal-mining town of about 1500 people, a town that no longer exists, was almost solidly black in its con-stituency. Moreover, the minstrel, either a white or a black in "blackface" makeup, consisting of black greasepaint applied to most of the face with large white ovals around the eyes and mouth, was fairly common. Historians note the popularity of the minstrel show, with its parade down Main Street, its chorus line of tambourine-equipped blackfaces, its interlocutor or straight man in the center, its Sambo and Mr. Bones at the ends.

This popularity began to decline in the 1920s with the inclusion of white scantily costumed chorus girls, but it took a sharp upswing with the advent of the "talkies" and nationwide radio programs. Minstrel shows were heard on the radio, and Micky Rooney and Judy Garland performed in an elaborately costumed minstrel show in *Babes on Broadway,* an act that was included later in *That's Entertainment* (M-G-M). Eddie Cantor and Al Jolson were nationally famous for their blackface singing, dancing, and comedy. In recent years there has been a reaction to this form of entertainment on the grounds that it

MEDICINE MEN: REMINISCENCES

degrades the black. Al Jolson's elaborate "Going to Heaven on a Mule" number is frequently cut from the film in which it plays a major part—if the film is shown at all.

James Stevens, who created a wide reputation for himself as publisher of Paul Bunyan folklore and author of novels about lumbering, was born near Albia in 1892 and lived in Moravia with his mother from 1897 to 1902. In the 1920s and 1930s he used those years as a basis for a half dozen wildly funny tales of life in Moravia that were published in H. L. Mencken's *American Mercury*. Stevens died in 1972.

TWO OF THE grandest giants of my boyhood were Dr. Benjamin Bearpaw and the Rev. Pearl Yates. The former was the sole proprietor of Dr. Bearpaw's Prairie Root for Kidney Trouble and the magnate of a glittering medicine show. The latter was the powerful Methodist minister in Moravia, the little Iowa town in which I lived as a boy. Near the end of my eighth year the two giants clashed in a fray which rocked Moravia to its roots.

The deep cause of the feud lay in the kidney trouble of the Rev. Mr. Yates. For many a year he had been afflicted with a malady which mystified all the regular doctors for miles around, so he had come to rely on treating himself, depending mainly on Peruna and Hostetter's Family Bitters. He turned to Prairie Root, so he declared, because he had grown certain that his trouble was in the kidneys. Soon he was telling all who inquired about his health that Prairie Root was toning up his system as it had never been toned up before, and he hailed Dr. Benjamin Bearpaw as a benefactor of humanity.

At this time the Rev. Yates held strong hopes of bringing the Bearpaw family into the Methodist fold. Dr. Bearpaw had just bought the Sol Taylor place on the south border of town, paying spot cash and showing so many other signs of wealth that he was invited to join the Odd Fellows. But the doctor held off, strictly minding his own business. An old Moravian church stood on the Taylor place, and he turned it into a medicine-making plant. On the door he posted a big sign which read:

BEARPAW LABORATORIES.
NO ADMITTANCE.
THIS MEANS YOU!!!

After his wife and five children were settled in their new home, Dr. Bearpaw returned to his traveling show. He left his family in charge of one John Badax, his handy man, who looked and acted so much like a scalping Indian of the Wild West that even the nosiest boys of the neighborhood shied away from the place.

But the Rev. Yates was bound to bring Mrs. Bearpaw and her children into the fold. For a month he called twice a week on the family, declaring that his labors would surely bear fruit. He bought a full six-bottle course of Prairie Root and sang the praises of the medicine far and wide. All Moravia agreed that it was mighty, mighty hard to skin around the Rev. Yates.

But then, after the doctor had been home on a Sunday visit, the minister was suddenly ordered off the premises by John Badax, and straightway he began to show his claws. First, he murmured against Prairie Root, vowing that he had been deceived. He solemnly declared that the third bottle had caused him to get up in the night more than ever. For a while he rested on this warning note. He called no more on Mrs. Bearpaw, but he did not speak against her. Apparently, he still had hope. It lasted until Dr. Bearpaw brought his medicine show to Moravia in late Summer, to put on a grand performance in his new home town.

In this performance, alas, Dr. Bearpaw lowered himself to the class of Tunk Chambers, the beer-drinking and card-playing barber, and Pleas Repp, the infidel liveryman. So he became a marked man among the Methodists of Moravia.

II

The show was held at a corner of the town square. It was a sultry night, with never a whisper from the maples and elms in the park. The hitching rack was lined with horses and rigs which smelled of sweat and the Summer prairie. Clover and straw padded the wagon beds. The horses stamped, switched and snorted, making their harness jingle. Every so often a hound would yap from a wagon.

At the main corner of the square torches flared. They shone over a big turnout of men and boys. I enjoyed the crowd tremendously: its manners were so free and easy. All about me men were chawing, smoking pipes, codding each other, roaring over their own jokes. The ribald Tunk Chambers was himself as good as a show.

But there was also a strong sober element in the crowd. Some of Moravia's most prominent citizens, such as U. G. Todd, our biggest grocer, Jeff Biggle, the shoe merchant, and Solon Shinkle, the hog-buyer and mayor, were on hand. I heard them agreeing that Dr. Benjamin Bearpaw was a great credit to Moravia, for every bottle of Prairie Root had BEARPAW LABORATORIES, MORAVIA, IOWA, in big letters on the label, and the medicine was so generally healing and comforting to the kidneys that it made the soundest kind of advertisement for the town. Mayor Shinkle said that he knew of at least five sufferers from kidney trouble who had been given up by Dr. Prouty, and all had begun to enjoy regular sleep since taking Prairie Root. The mayor predicted that Doan's

". . . the two giants clashed in a fray which rocked Moravia to its roots."

After sketches by Richard Harsh of Moravia's town square

Kidney Pills would rot on the shelves from now on, so far as Moravia was concerned, and U. G. Todd and Mr. Biggle agreed.

The crowd hushed as a handsome young man stepped from the hind end of a huge covered wagon. The stage was a plain platform flanked by carbide torches. Standing out in the white blaze, the handsome young man was dazzling in a shiny plug hat and a suit with brown-and-red checks almost a foot square. He set his hat, top down, on a small table and foamed into a mighty speech about the world-famous splendors of Dr. Bearpaw's Nonpareil Medicine Show. Then the fun started, and it was so fast that I could remember it afterward only in a sort of shining haze. Never before had I reveled in such a feast, and all of it was flavored with music and song.

The first-act prodigy was performed by a minstrel who sneaked out from the wagon and poured a pitcher of water into the handsome young man's plug hat. I almost died from holding in the laughs, so as not to give the joke away, until the young man finished his speech, yanked up his hat with a flourish and jammed it on his head. He simply soused himself, and there he stood, petrified with amazement, while water streamed all over him. And didn't everybody just double up, rip loose and howl, though! I hadn't laughed so hard in a coon's age.

Then the acts came on so fast that I could only gape in joy and wonder. The minstrel shot out on the platform with a banjo, and he fairly tore the strings off the instrument as he roared such coon songs as "I Got Mine" and "Goo-Goo Eyes," doing shuffles and hoe-downs with every chorus. After a half-dozen of them, another minstrel joined him, and a body could have dropped me with a feather when I realized that he was the handsome young man, all blacked up and in dry clothes. The two minstrels snapped and snarled at each other for a spell, cracking a killing joke every time; then they took up mandolins, turned solemn, and rendered several sad duets. They sang "Hello, Central, Give Me Heaven," in such a heart-wringing style that it was hard to believe they had been full of nothing but wit and humor a spell back.

The crowd was properly primed with sentiment when Dr. Bearpaw himself strode forth soberly in his Indian regalia. Indian war drums sounded from the gloom of the covered wagon, and with them shivery yells. I was deeply stirred. Dr. Bearpaw was a mighty sight there in his beaded buckskin uniform, his head plumed with colored eagle feathers, his face streaked with war paint, a tomahawk in one hand and a bottle of Prairie Root for Kidney Trouble in the other. He set the bottle on the table, stuck the tomahawk in his belt, then stood and stared over the crowd. The drums beat on, but softer now, and the yells whined away.

Even Tunk Chambers hearkened soberly as Dr. Bearpaw began to expound the woes of the noble Red man. The speech was mournful in its first part, with its sad pictures of poor Lo being hounded from pillar to post by ravenous whites, starving and freezing, having nowhere to lay his weary head. Such pictures would have left the people feeling miserably sorry for the abused Red man, had it not been for what Dr. Bearpaw called the silver lining. The Indian's life did have a bright side, the doctor admitted, in a cheerier tone. The brightness was the amazing health poor Lo enjoyed; and he enjoyed it purely and simply because he kept his kidneys toned up night and day with Prairie Root. Dr. Bearpaw went on to show that all mortal ills, even rheumatism and consumption, started from kidney trouble.

"Stay the evil at its source!" he roared. "That's one lesson the smartest white man can learn from the poor Indian of the plains!"

Long ago, said the doctor, he had made up his mind to forgive his white brothers and share with them the main medicine secret of the Cherokee tribe. He then ripped out with some hair-raising stories about his narrow escapes from Cherokee chiefs, acting them out with blood-curdling yells and frightful swings of tomahawk and Bowie knife. The Cherokee chiefs were all revengeful, Dr. Bearpaw said when he had calmed down; they would have been pleased pink to see the kidneys of all palefaces go to rack and ruin; but not him, not Dr. Benjamin Bearpaw, who had a bigger vision.

"Whatever ails you, my white brothers, my paleface friends," orated the doctor, in his deepest tones, "be certain and sure that this here miracle tonic and balm, this here magic elixir supreme, will tone you up! One bottle for a dollar, and one bottle will start you on the road to health! Six bottles for five dollars, and you have nature's own complete cure for all the ills that flesh is heir to! Prairie Root is warranted. Prairie Root stands the test. It reaches the spot. Ask any Bearpaw patient. Why, I can show you testimonials—"

Right there Tunk Chambers had to horn in.

"How about Rev. Yates, doc?" the barber yelled. "He took three bottles of this here Prairie Root of yourn, and he claims ever since he's more out of bed than in it of a night. He vows Prairie Root is only fit for a owl!"

The sinful element in the crowd set up a laugh. Its leaders, Tunk Chambers and Pleas Repp, were always taking digs at the kinds of medicine the Rev. Yates tried on his trouble. Dr. Bearpaw would have done well to gloss this one over. But he was ignorant of the immense power of the Methodist minister in the town, and he tore loose.

"The Rev. Yates never had no kidney trouble, my good friend," he boomed, his black eyes snapping. "If he did, Prairie Root would have toned his kidneys up, you can bet your bottom dollar! Saint or sinner, Prairie Root never fails to stop 'em from getting up in the night. Let Rev. Yates swig Peruna and Hostetter's to his heart's content. Let him likewise keep his mouth shut about Prairie Root, for in the great field of internal medicine the Rev. Pearl Yates is as ignorant as a suckling babe!''

The sinful element whooped and cheered, and Tunk and Pleas led the buying as Dr. Bearpaw's helpers sold through the crowd. But the prominent citizens shook their heads ruefully.

"That was mighty pore business," I heard Mayor Shinkle say. "Mighty pore. Dr. Bearpaw went a mite too fur, you ask me. This'll raise a stink in Moravy, see if it don't."

It did, but only under cover for several months. Dr. Bearpaw took a Fall and Winter trip into the South, where kidney trouble was raging, leaving his family in the care of John Badax again. The two children, Grover Cleveland Bearpaw and his sister Eunice, were old enough to attend school. They were mannerly and bright and gave the family a kind name. But by the end of Winter gossip about Mrs. Bearpaw and John Badax was creeping around.

III

Early in April the doctor returned. The next morning after his arrival I went uptown with my grandmother to shop at Todd's grocery. As we neared the main corner of the square I noticed a pack of men in a circle. In their midst the Rev. Pearl Yates and Dr. Benjamin Bearpaw stood face to face. The doctor wore a Bryan hat, a cutaway coat and a gates-ajar collar, but I had never seen him look more like a savage. He spoke low to the Rev. Yates, his tone sounding like a case-knife scraped on a joint of stovepipe.

"I'll rend and tear you into bloody bits with my bare hands," he rasped. "With my bare hands, Rev. Yates, for one more whisper. Another single whisper against my wife, Rev. Yates, and you'll be rent and tore like a serpent in a eagle's claws!"

"You've mistaken me," the Rev. Yates muttered hoarsely through his black beard. "I declare you shorely have mistaken me, sir!"

Grandma hustled me on. Her eyes snapped pleasantly, for she was the only Hardshell Baptist in town, and the Rev. Yates was always nagging her about changing to his church.

The jawing between the minister and the doctor, it appeared, ended without an actual fight. Mayor Shinkle was called, and he managed to patch up the trouble for the time. The Moravia people generally were cautious in talking about the matter. The doctor had stirred some fear in them, but the Rev. Yates was too strong in those days to be spoken against openly by any but the sinful element. For he had just bagged the famous Hinote brothers for a union camp-meeting revival. It was a mighty triumph. Never before had the Rev. Noah Hinote and the Rev. Sad Sam Hinote conducted a revival in so small a town.

On the first Sunday night after the jawing the Methodist church was packed to the rafters. The Rev. Yates had announced as his subject,

"Secret Sins of Moravia; or, Let Us Bring Light Into the Hell-Holes." The revival was to start in two weeks. The minister promised to unfold the works of Satan in Moravia, so that all in town would realize the tremendous need for the Hinote brothers.

My grandmother predicted that he would use their sermons to further his feud with Dr. Bearpaw, and she was right. The doctor was also raising a stir as he made his plans for the Spring circuit. His first move was to organize a baseball team and call it the Moravia Bearpaws. He then arranged for a season of Sunday games with the teams of Mystic, Iconium, Tyrone, Albia, and other small neighboring towns. For the first time in Moravia's history the sinful element came out brazenly in the open, with Tunk Chambers and Pleas Repp vowing they would support baseball on the Sabbath in spite of Hell and high water. Even U. G. Todd and Jeff Biggle ventured to speak in favor of the move, and Mayor Shinkle did not speak against it. The Moravia Methodists had a real fight on their hands.

So the feud between the Rev. Yates and Dr. Bearpaw began to spread through the town, with the church people lining up on one side, the sinful element on the other, and some of the leading merchants squirming in the middle. Soon Dr. Bearpaw was more than holding his own. But the Rev. Yates still looked unbeatable as he stood in his pulpit that Sunday night and turned the searchlight on Moravia's secret sins.

He always made his congregation feel that he knew a mighty lot more than he ever told. Every sermon was primed with warnings about thieves in the night, wolves in sheep's clothing, snakes in the grass, and spiders in dark corners. The Rev. Yates never used names, even when preaching against the card-playing and beer-drinking that went on in the hall above Tunk Chambers' barber shop, or the infidelity on tap in Pleas Repp's livery barn, but his hints always made plain what sinner he was reviling. On this Sunday night he had not preached five minutes before his congregation understood that he was exposing the old Moravian church as the town's vilest hell-hole, and Dr. Bearpaw as the worst shape of Satan we had.

His voice rose in a hoarse rumble. He whaled the pulpit with a hairy fist.

"Satan's vilest and rottenest poison is rum!" roared the Rev. Yates. "Wine is a mocker, strong drink is ragin', but medicine can be, and often is, the Devil's foulest, filthiest, stinkin'est deceit and snare! Ah, my Chrischun friends, well do I know whereof I speak! I don't need to tell you how sorely afflicted I have been in all my years here. Let me tell you that likewise have I been sorely deceived. It has been said by a man who thinks he is too big for Moravy that your pastor is as igner'nt of medicine as a sucklin' babe. In a humble Chrischun sperit, I admit it is likely so. But one thing I do know," roared the Rev. Yates, sawing the air, "and that is a certain medicine which is claimed to be a elixir for the kidneys is nothin' but a filthy, scummy, stinkin' lie! A Devil's foul lie in a bottle, my Chrischun friends! And I declare that this here black, slimy viper which Moravy cherishes in her fair bosom is the lowest, filthiest secret sin Moravy knows! Ain't it time here for the holy Hinote brothers? In the name of the Lord, I ask you ag'in, ain't it time?''

With that, the Rev. Yates cooled down, to let his hints soak into the congregation. They didn't need much soaking. Never before had he made his meaning so plain. In all the pews heads nodded furiously together, and whispering rose like swarming bees. The Rev. Yates hauled out a bandanna, mopped his sweating face, and stared over the congregation with the most pleased expression I had ever seen on him. He failed to turn on any more fireworks until the end of his sermon, but filled in with stories that had good morals.

They were mainly about himself. One told of the time he had tried cubeb cigarettes for a cold, and so risked being caught in the filthiest and most godless form of the tobacco habit. In another time of mortal weakness he had learned to play Authors, and later was vilely tempted to take up games with gambling cards. There was also a story about chawing tobacco for the toothache. Then the Rev. Yates swung back to an account of his trouble, and in telling of all the medicines he had tried, he led up to another roaring blast against Prairie Root.

''Ag'in I trusted like the innocent sucklin' babe I am said to be,'' he roared. ''And ag'in I awoke to find myself bein' licked by the forked tongue of the old serpent. Too many in Moravy have not awoke. Too many in Moravy are still weak enough to want to take a certain rich man into that lodge of fine, upstandin' Chrischuns, the Odd Fellows. It is indeed time here for the Hinote brothers. In a humble Chrischun sperit I shall leave to them the righteous work of crushin' the viper that pollutes Moravy's fair bosom.''

After services the commotion was like that of a crowd leaving a circus. The Rev. Yates stood in the vestibule, shaking hands. The people milled around him, buzzing with questions and straining ears as they crowded to the doors.

Then every tongue was suddenly hushed and every eye was staring wide. For into the light of the vestibule pressed Tunk Chambers, with fat Pleas Repp red and puffing behind him. They were a staggering sight to all the church people—at least Tunk was. Pleas often attended church, and had been converted four times, and would quit a horse-trade to argue religion, but Tunk was an abandoned and defiant sinner. I stood back with my grandmother and marveled at him now. A big, raw-boned, sandy-haired young man, his freckled face usually shone with good nature. But now his freckles blazed and he spoke in a snarl.

''So that's what you call religion,'' snarled Tunk Chambers, squaring off before the Rev. Yates. ''Pertendin' to visit a pore Injun woman to convert her, and you go prowlin' into her husband's business while he's out tryin' to relieve the sick an' make a decent livin' for his fambly! Go ahead, Rev. Yates, if that's what you call religion! There's more and more in Moravy who would call it—''

But Tunk Chambers got no further. By this time the Methodist men were growling in wrath and closing upon him. They surely would have laid violent hands on him if Mayor Solon Shinkle hadn't stepped in and threatened him with arrest.

"Never mind," said Tunk. "I'm goin'. Goin' straight to my shop for some bay rum to kill this here smell."

He was grinning again as he pushed out through the wrathful and scandalized crowd. The Rev. Yates had not said a word. His face was white as death above his black beard and he got away from the packed vestibule in no more than a minute.

"It's my trouble grippin' me ag'in," he excused himself. "I must get home for some medicine. The sperit has had its say through me. The rest is up to the good Lord and the Hinote brothers."

Out on the street corner Tunk and Pleas had a regular mob around them, all cheering and laughing. Moravia's sinful element was on the warpath at last.

IV

The Rev. Yates' bold sermon and the barber's brazen defiance turned the town upside down. With all the church people up in arms and a big revival looming, the merchants, excepting Jeff Biggle, inclined to the side of the minister. I listened eagerly to all the arguments I could hear, and finally it was plain to me that the Rev. Yates had somehow learned a lot that was sinister and fascinating about Dr. Bearpaw's medicine in the times he called on the family and bought so many bottles. But he refused to utter another word against the doctor. The sperit had had its say, he kept repeating, and the outcome lay with the Lord. He still had hopes, he declared, that Dr. Bearpaw would come to see the light before it was too late. All week the town wondered just what he had up his sleeve.

The doctor was out on a trip with his show and did not return to Moravia until Sunday. In the meantime Tunk Chambers had the baseball team, of which he was pitcher and captain, out practicing furiously every day. The barber bragged all over that Iconium would be played in Moravia on the Sabbath in spite of Hell and high water. The Rev. Yates made no open move against the game, but a Methodist and United Brethren committee called on Mayor Solon Shinkle and demanded that he stop the desecration. The mayor shuffled the committee off and sneaked away on a hog-buying trip.

The game was played, and the sinful element swarmed in force to the diamond near the Milwaukee depot. Dr. Bearpaw drove in with the Iconium team. He appeared before the crowd in high dignity, wearing his cutaway coat and Bryan hat, and the section-hands, teamsters, coal-miners, farm-laborers, town roustabouts, and others of Moravia's lost souls gave the doctor as many rousing cheers as they raised for his ball team. The Moravia Bearpaws won the game by a lop-sided score, and Jeff Biggle and U. G. Todd were yelling as loudly as the section-hands when it ended. Dr. Bearpaw appeared to be holding his own with the Rev. Yates.

But after the game there were queer doings. Dr. Bearpaw and Tunk Chambers had a long and solemn confab by themselves, and then the doctor drove directly to the Methodist parsonage. In no time the news was all over town, but nobody could find out what happened when the two giants met. Dr. Bearpaw drove home from the parsonage like fury, shut himself up with his family, and left early on Monday morning for his circuit. At the Sunday night services the Rev. Yates disappointed the congregation that jammed the Methodist church by preaching a weak sermon about the evils of Romanism and infidelity in Moravia, and never uttering a sound about Dr. Bearpaw. But at the end of his sermon he promised Moravia the surprise of its life at the opening revival service. He made the promise in his most mysterious style, and would say no more. But everybody was sure and certain that the surprise would concern Dr. Bearpaw, and a tremendous blowup was expected.

I attended the first meeting of the revival with my grandmother. As soon as we reached the grove I was struck by a circus feeling. Lanterns were strung on the trees along the road and the big tent was all a-shine from the lamps inside. Before the entrance families gathered in a jumbled crowd, which was sort of oozing into the tent. Farm people were still driving up in rigs. A wagon would clatter to the hitching rack, yells of "Whoaah!" "Back up, Baldy, you!" "Gee, Buck!" would cut through the excited hum of the crowd's talk, and in a minute the farm family would be just another part of the squeezing mob. A good many Hardshell farmers were attending. Grandma kept holding me back to neighbor with them, until I was certain we would never get a seat. But we did, half-way up the rows of benches.

Coal-oil lamps with monster tin reflectors hung from the tent top and a string of them blazed over the preaching platform. Two strangers were seated among the Moravia ministers. One had his head bowed in a kind of brooding prayer. Every so often his bony shoulders would heave in the mournfulest sigh. I grew certain that he was the Rev. Sad Sam Hinote, whose stories of drunken fathers and songs of broken hearts were known to wring tears from a stone. The other was a gaunt, glowering man with a bush of red hair, a ragged sandy beard, and such monster freckles on his hands that I could make out each one from where I sat. He would surely be the Rev. Noah Hinote, the Sledge-hammer Revivalist, as the Rev. Yates had called him. The Hinotes, it appeared, had been born in Ireland. They were orphans, for their father had been a Methodist missionary in County Cork, and died of it. The Rev. Noah was famous for his fist fights with atheists who tried to break up his revivals.

Moravia's sinful element was out in a body, I soon noticed, and its members had never appeared more brazen and bold. The Rev. Yates had hardly finished the opening prayer before they started cutting up. They got worse when the congregation arose to sing. When the hymn, "At the Cross" was given I could plainly hear Tunk Chambers singing, "At the bar, at the bar, where I smoked my first cigar, and the money in my pockets rolled away, hallelujah!" instead of the proper sacred words. The church people glared in a red fury at the sinners, who only grinned back. Trouble was smoldering.

V

But the Rev. Noah Hinote seemed to be paying it no heed as he launched into the opening orgies of the camp-meeting. In a voice that rasped like a buzz saw to all quarters of the tent, he announced that his first three sermons in Moravia would deal with missionarying to the heathen. One would deal with the papist Irish, and another would tell of the progress of the Word among the heathen Chinese, but tonight's sermon, account of a special request from the Rev. Pearl Yates, would have to do with missionary labors among the savage Indians of the Wild West. He would show a powerful lesson in the three sermons, said the Rev. Noah; namely, that hosts of heathen had seen the light of the Gospel, and if the least of these could see it, surely the civilized and intelligent folks of Moravia could not fail.

The announcement caused a violent stir. All the Moravians in the congregation saw the shrewd hand of the Rev. Yates in tonight's sermon on the Indians. He smiled through his beard there, as though he were sitting down to fried chicken. Tunk Chambers and his friends were a bit sobered. They waited solemnly for the sermon.

It was a rip-roarer from the start. The Rev. Yates, for all his power, could never hold a candle to the Rev. Noah Hinote. In the first ten minutes the revivalist whooped it up harder against Rome and Rum than our Methodist minister had done all Winter. It appeared that the Indians of the West had been harder to convert than any other breed of heathen, for Roman priests had worked on them first, and then infidel traders had mired them in drunken despair.

"I been there, I've seen, and I know!" the Rev. Noah screamed, his face running sweat, his eyes glittering, and his red hair standing up like fire in a draft. "Down in the Territory I have walked among the horrible evils that was wrought. Hearken well now, while I expound unto you a parable of the miser'ble sinful state of the heathen Cherokees!"

Every ear in the congregation stood out quivering. Hardly a soul seemed to breathe as the Rev. Noah sawed and roared on in his parable. It was a story about a little missionary school in the Cherokee nation, and of a beautiful young Cherokee woman who brought her papoose there to learn the Christian life. That was the main point, but the Rev. Noah threw in Wild West stories on the side which beat anything I had ever read in Diamond Dick. He made the bloodiest pictures of scalping parties creeping out from the campfires and tepees at night, crawling up on the sleeping emigrant train, and then slaughtering the poor whites like cattle. He next pictured the camp again and its bloody revels, the Indians dancing with the dripping scalps, all raging from the poison of Hell which the sinful traders had sold them. Finally, the Rev. Noah fetched the young Christian Cherokee woman on the scene; and he made the most pitiful picture of her trying to put a stop to the drinking and dancing, until a chief knocked her down, leaving her to bleed and suffer for hours. Yet she would not give up, and her courage won many Cherokees for the true church. She brought her boy up to lead a holy life.

"But it was all in vain," cried the Rev. Noah in lamenting tones. "When the boy was growed, the sinful traders lured him away by use of the Rum Demon. In spite of all his mother's prayers and tears he run off and used the education the school had learnt him to get a job in a white man's medicine show. Like that he done, leavin' his Chrischun mother to grieve and mourn. Can't you see that mother—oh, can't you see that mother!—heartsick and a-mournin' afore her tepee there, prayin' to the good Lord to fetch her errin' and wanderin' son back from the dark ha'nts of sin? Oh, can't you see that mother—can't you see that pore mother now—"

The revivalist was making a chant of his sermon, his gaunt body swaying, his huge hands sawing the congregation into time with the chant. Then guitar music strummed out and the Rev. Sad Sam Hinote began to sing. He sang "Where Is My Wandering Boy Tonight?" in the most heart-rending tenor I had ever heard. At every pause in the music the Rev. Noah would grip his hands to Heaven and heave a rasping moan, "Oh, pray for that pore mother!" By the time the first chorus had quavered out, sobs were breaking in every part of the congregation. Even Tunk Chambers was licking dry lips.

As the song ended, moaned and whispered prayers came from every bench.

"Think of that pore mother!" cried the revivalist again. "Think of how you might be her errin' and wanderin' child, and if you was, how you would shorely come forward now. Oh!—oh, that pore mother!"

"Come to Jesus! Come to Jesus!" wailed the tenor voice of the Rev.

Sad Sam Hinote. Then his brother's thundering bass harmonized along: "Come to Jesus!" Sinners began to rise.

Then the big surprise that the Rev. Yates had promised struck the camp-meeting like heat-lightning. From the shadows of the tent wall at the entrance a rich voice boomed like a bell in a glory-shout. The people, startled, turned to look. A gasp as big as a wind blowing through trees filled the tent. For down the center aisle marched Dr. Benjamin Bearpaw, shining in his grandest Indian regalia, his colored eagle feathers gleaming and waving in the yellow lamplight.

VI

Arms folded, head high, the doctor marched with the tread of a drum-major for the mourner's bench. The astounded congregation sat like lumps of stone. The Rev. Yates stepped forward with a yell that split the quiet like an ax:

"Here's the surprise I promised! Here's the son of that pore mother, come forward to confess his sins and be born again!"

Then the minister reached down and drew the doctor to the platform beside him. The Rev. Sad Sam Hinote shrieked a song of salvation. The Rev. Noah bawled praises to the Lord. Frenzy struck the congregation. The benches heaved and tumbled from the leaps of exalted saints, and the howls of smitten sinners billowed the tent-top and shook the swinging lamps. On the preaching platform the United Brethren, Cumberland Presbyterian and Campbellite ministers joined in the yells of the Rev. Noah, but the Rev. Yates was at peace. He embraced his enemy and bowed his head in prayer. Dr. Bearpaw stood with his own arms still folded, staring out at the congregation.

Mayor Solon Shinkle rose from beside U. G. Todd and Jeff Biggle.

"That settles Tunk Chambers," I heard him say to them. "I knowed the sinful element could never skin around the Rev. Pearl Yates."

The uproar lasted for a mighty long spell. At least fifty sinners crowded forward, while the saints howled in jubilation from the benches. Whenever the fever began to cool, the Rev. Noah would hoist glory-shouts again, while his sad brother sang rousing hymns. Mayor Shinkle stood on the platform now, backing up the Methodist minister. I kept looking and wondering at Tunk Chambers and Pleas Repp. They would gaze up at Dr. Bearpaw, then stare at each other, and break into the craziest chuckles and grins. I began to suspect, boy though I was, that they had cooked up something. Soon I was so sure of it and so curious that I ceased to be stirred by the uprising of the spirit.

At last the Rev. Noah calmed the congregation down and announced that Dr. Bearpaw would now confess his sins and give testimony. As the congregation settled to hearken, the doctor shook off the Rev. Yates and stepped forward in the flourishing style he used in his medicine show.

"I am speaking short and plain," boomed Dr. Bearpaw in his richest voice. "The surprise you have witnessed, the parable you were told, and me coming forward in the rig of a Cherokee chief *are all a trap I baited for the Hinote brothers and the Rev. Pearl Yates!* The trap is sprung and their hypocrisy has found them out!"

The people were petrified. Along every bench eyes bugged unwinkingly and mouths gaped open. The holy men on the platform stared in stark quiet. The brow of the Rev. Pearl Yates was like snow and shone with sudden sweat. The doctor boomed on:

"While Rev. Yates preached religion to my family, he spied around for a club to hold over my head. He was sure he found it, but not until he was backed by these here Hinotes did he dast to come into the open with the threat. You all know the sermon he preached against the biggest sinner in your town. You all know nobody but Dr. Benjamin Bearpaw was meant. And you all know that I faced this preacher in his home. There the Rev. Yates charged me with keeping barrels of whiskey under the floor of the old church for the making of Prairie Root. He swore to have me jugged as an Indian dealing in ardent spirits unless I came to time—"

"And for jest that you *will* be jugged!" the Rev. Noah Hinote found his tongue at last.

"There's the ketch!" roared the doctor gloatingly. "There's the ketch in it. Fact is, I've nary a drop of Indian blood! I'm half Spanish and half Mormon, a native son of Utah Territory; I married a Cherokee princess from the circus show of Buffalo Bill Cody; and I'm licensed by the U.S. Gover'ment to make whiskey-medicine for Methodist hypocrites like the Rev. Pearl Yates! Yes, sir, I can show you my papers. The Rev. Yates vowed to take me to his bosom if I'd go through with a conversion, and I baited the trap. Here I confess, and if it ruins me in Ioway, let 'er ruin. Dr. Benjamin Bearpaw has smote his enemies with the jawbone of an ass, and he's plenty satisfied!"

The doctor dropped nimbly off the platform and started down the aisle. The Rev. Noah Hinote foamed after him. Other saints sprang into the charge. For a spell there was a raving riot at the back of the tent, as Tunk Chambers heaved in with the sinful element. By the time the mayor and the prominent citizens had restored order the Rev. Yates had fallen in a sickness and had to be packed home.

VII

It was the end of the feud between Dr. Benjamin Bearpaw and the Rev. Pearl Yates in Moravia. Their labors in the town were also done. The minister was actually smitten with kidney trouble at last, and he left for the cure at Hot Springs, Arkansas. There he took a call to another vineyard. Dr. Bearpaw sold out and moved to what he called the more fruitful field of Kansas. The story of the revival had spread to the neighboring counties, and in them his Indian orations could no longer go over. The Rev. Noah Hinote was laid up with a wrenched back from his fight with Tunk Chambers, but the scandal would have ruined the revival anyhow. The sinful element was in the saddle. In the Fall election Mayor Solon Shinkle was retired to his hog-buying business, and Jeff Biggle, who had never joined a church, was voted into the job.

So one of Moravia's mightiest times ended.

"Never seen the beat of it," agreed the old men of the town. "Even the Hayes-Tilden election never raised sech a stink in Moravy as that there feud between Dr. Bearpaw and the Rev. Pearl Yates."

🌸 🌸 Phil Stong

IF IT MAY be said that some people are "born with a silver spoon in their mouth," it may be said of Phil Stong that he was born with a golden tongue in his cheek! For example, the introduction to *If School Keeps* (1940) from which "Matriculation" is taken, begins with:

NOTICE
If any accounts of places, persons or incidents in this book resemble any actual places, persons, incidents or names, my memory has improved, and I am delighted.

This same lighthearted air informs all the book and gives Stong's piece about his going-to-school days in 1904 in Keosauqua, down in Van Buren County in the big bend of the Des Moines River (Stong called the area "Pittsville" in his fiction), a pleasant quality that makes it sheer delight to read—even though it may turn off some who long for what the Nobel Prize people call "djupinis" (profundity).

His great-grandfather settled in Van Buren County in 1837. Stong fictionalized his coming in *Buckskin Breeches* (1937). Stong came along in 1899. For awhile he taught school—Biwabik, Minnesota, on the iron range; Neodesha, Kansas, in the oil country; and at Drake University where he got his degree. While working for the *Des Moines Register,* he met and married novelist Virginia Swain.

Keosauqua in 1904 was somewhat larger than it is today, somewhat over a thousand. Because it had once been a station on the Underground Railroad, it had a fair proportion of blacks. Westward-bound Yankees and Germans from the northeast had settled here, intermingling with hill people from the south. Stong has shown the consequences of this intermingling in *The Rebellion of Lenny Barlow* (1937), a novel about a hill-country boy in a society of Yankees and Germans.

Stong's first novel, *State Fair* (1932), brought him instant fame and wealth and started him on a career as novelist, author of children's books, historian of sorts (*Hawkeyes,* 1940), and autobiographer. He published more than forty books, including one on horses, *Horses and Americans* (1939). *State Fair* was filmed on three occasions, the first time with Will Rogers; his *Career* was filmed also. He died in 1957.

MATRICULATION

ON A SEPTEMBER day in 1904 my mother kissed me goodbye, and I went stumbling off with a slate, a "Big Chief" tablet and a ten-cent pencil-box to the old two-storey brick school on the hill. Father had moved to town from the farm particularly for the sake of my education, and except for Brown Manning and George ("Pot") Kittle, who were across-the-street neighbors, I was as much a stranger as if I had just dropped in from Mars.

I had never seen so many kids together in one place in my life as there were in the big schoolyard. They scared me pink. I moved cautiously around the edge of the yard and slid in the front door, avoiding the pump and water bench and the side door where the men in the Third Grade and the upstairs High School were privileged to enter. The first bell rang at 8:30, the second at 8:45, and the last bell five minutes before nine. During this twenty-five-minute period I sat at a double desk, envying the sophistication of all the little city devils—Keosauqua had over 1400 people then—who came in, recognized each other and put their books away. The most sophisticated, of course, were a few little cretins who had failed to make their first two grades in the preceding year and were back in the same room again.

I did not know this and would not have understood it if I had. They were all Plato to me. The hellish little girls looked at me contemptuously as I sat peering like an imbecile at my empty slate; the little boys gave me the odd fishy gaze which is diplomatic and conventional between animals whose capacities for licking or being licked are still unknown.

Miss Snyder, who had taught my mother in the same room, kept her attention on paper work till the third bell rang; then she told me to go out and line up with the double rank of not unusually horrible brats who would march into the building and split files to their rooms when the monitor of the day blew on a little police whistle. I had to fall in toward the end of the line, of course, which would have automatically classified me as a tough character, except for the fact that I was so obviously uncertain and creaky. Despicable maidens were fighting for places in the front of the line, in a ladylike way; the fairly good little boys, the average little boys, and most particularly the bad little boys had come to the slaughter with less ostensible eagerness.

Debonair high-school students passed our wavering lines with hauteur and went into the building just like people going into a building. We were given a step rhythm and marched into the long hall, where we separated into four branches, for the four rooms that took care of seven grades. In the Primary Room—First and Second Grades—we were seated with great promptness, the goody-goody girls grabbing the front seats and the vilest little boys the rear corner seats. As soon as they were transposed by Miss Snyder we plunged into song, beginning with "Jesus Wants Me for a Sunbeam," which Jesus most certainly did not, unless His wits were wandering. Afterward we intoned the sentiment that we were all little jewels in Jesus' crown and then we got down to business with,

> Hold your hands if they are clean,
> By your teacher to be seen . . .

to the leading theme in Haydn's Surprise Symphony. All the little girls' hands were clean and all the little boys' hands were grubby from the exercises and occupations of the playground. Two or three of the dirtiest boys were sent as examples out to the pump, where the janitor kept a basin and a cake of soap for the use of the shameful ones.

While they were gone they were further penalized by missing the morning reading, a come-on as carefully planned as a serial could be by Ruby Ayres or Ethel Dell to stop at a high point at the end of each instalment. Some months later Miss Snyder had the bad luck to read from a volume of *Chatterbox* that was also in my library, and part of my play period was spent every morning—and my social prestige, never too high, greatly enhanced—by my daily recitals of what had been read and what was coming next to my little playmates who had played hooky or planned to play hooky that day. Mother had taught me to read in my third year; I was a consummate introvert and a sissy of high degree—an oldest child brought up in a virtually boyless village, till we moved to town—but my literary abilities frequently saved my life from the large roughnecks of the hooky-playing classes.

After the reading we got down to the business of the day. Children of our time and place usually knew their alphabets and how to print block letters when they started to school; the simplest addition and subtraction are almost instinctive properties of the white race, though later readings in Frazer and Briffault have informed me that the concept of "ten" is as much beyond some primitives as the concept of the decimal system was beyond us; but all of us knew that if you took two pennies from ten pennies the remaining stake was one ice-cream soda and three hunks of taffy.

I started out that morning with aces, cards and spades scholastically, but, to mingle the diversions, eleven miles behind the eight ball socially. Dad had run a village store and I had the fundamentals of very simple mathematics; I watched the Second Grade struggling with short division with profound contempt. Mother had taught me to read by a system that did not become "modern" for twenty years or so; she drew circles around pictures and a line to the word representing the object. Her system of indicating verbs was used by the ancient Egyptians. An arrow pointing to a boy's feet reminded me that the word underlined was "run." Other parts of speech had simply to be memorized, but it is amazing how much of this kind of pabulum a mind with nothing much in it can absorb in a few

"I went stumbling off . . . to the old two-storey brick school on the hill."

PHIL STONG (THIRD FROM RIGHT, FRONT ROW) AND CLASSMATES, 1908.

months, and what I absorbed came to me as a complete image, so that the gruesome struggles of my little peers with *Pollard's Synthetic Reader* always seemed fantastically amusing, though sounding syllables at Miss Snyder's whim got to be a bore; however when Benny or Wheezy pronounced "tough," "tooj," or "below," "bellow," my laughter rang shrill and clear till they caught me that evening.

As the day wore on the room began to adopt its proper and conventional odor. It had been scrubbed, fumigated and disinfected in the summer, for those were the days when you could expect at least one school epidemic to relieve the tedium every winter—measles, whooping-cough, diphtheria, typhoid, smallpox, mumps. We had at least one of each during my school years, though we succeeded in burying only two of our associates in the ten years of my first sentence—they succumbed to diphtheria.

It took us a little better than half a day to conquer the original sanitary smells of the room. Then sweat and lunch-boxes took over where they had left off in June; two or three of the youngest children had the customary first-day accidents before they got it through their heads about raising their fingers; some of the little girls affected perfume; and the characteristic, indefinable musk of young children mingled with the dusty smell of chalk, mint from surreptitious and abandoned ruffians who were chewing gum on the sly—it was a symphony, of sorts, even though it had some modernistic sour notes.

In midmorning we had a "recess," distinguished by the fact that it was the most conspicuously strenuous part of the day. The girls retired to their special corner of the yard where, as far as I could ever see, they did nothing but gossip, but the boys started the season's first game of Blackman between two old trees which were "bases." The high-school men got up a little football practice out in the road, but the rest of us started running back and forth between the trees.

It was a great illustration of the power of the meek, for the first "it" was the last man into base, hence necessarily the party least fitted to be "it." But with every one running from base to base at once, at a signal the next poorest candidate for "it" would finally be caught and the two "its" would concentrate on another of the unfit. Then there would be three and shortly four or five, at which time these sheep would band together to get a lion. The lion would then proceed to knock off most favored lions while the sheep kept on capturing sheep, till there were too many of the weaker creatures, reenforced by the larger and faster boys, for even the swiftest runner to escape. The last man caught was "it" for the next game, which threw the whole procedure into a second cycle, for this last man would be formidable and would disdain lambs; in this phase the least desirable capture would be the last one and the game reverted to its original status. It was a small study in civilizations.

In order to legalize a capture the victim had to be patted on the back firmly three times, so that each occasion ended with a big tussle on the ground to get the prey turned over. This led to vital alterations in our costumes and general appearance, which probably distressed the teachers, but there was nothing they could do about it. Blackman was sacred on the campus.

Every year of my grade-school days I heard homilies on the wickedness of playing marbles for keeps, and every year every boy in the grades played marbles for keeps. After every snow we were told about the dangers of pneumonia and diphtheria—this was before influenza—and after every snow the whole yard patterned out into trodden, four-spoked wheels where we played Fox and Geese, exercising at top speed and doing everything in the way of wrestling around in the snow that we possibly could to give the little pneumococci as soft a home as possible. One of the boys finally did catch pneumonia, a very light case, but we deprecated this as playing into the teachers' hands.

Diphtheria was rather more serious; Howard Stull and Howard Haney died of it, and at various times several others got near enough to the pearly gates to read their names on the mailbox; I went through those years in the happy conviction that I could not catch the stuff because I had had my tonsils out.

Lunch time was the high social hour for the farm pupils. They ate their lunches on the lawn in good weather and off of their desks in bad, while the rest of us had commonplace meals at a table. It was not till I was ten years old that Grandfather's death thrust the administration of his farm on our family and made me a member in good standing of the lunch-box society and established in my mind forever the definitely superior quality of roast beef when eaten in the fingers, preferably dirty.

The primary grades were let out a little in advance of the high school so that none of us would be squashed by the boots of the brawny citizens from upstairs, creating a nuisance for the janitor. We formed in the aisles and marched out in good order to a spirited march from the parlor organ.

Fun! we thought, bursting into capers and whoops once we were down the steps. Poor little devils! We did not know that we were long-termers. Few of us were sprung short of ten years; some of us would, like Miss Snyder and Miss Hartson, mark all the rest of our lives, as did the famous Queen of Spain ("It's a hell of a life, said the Queen of Spain") by gestative periods of nine months, by class bells, by the smell of form-aldehyde and young bodies, by class desks and the unavoidable formulae of the classroom. Some of us would never get out; if I had known that my next twenty years would be principally active, between September and June, in one schoolhouse or another, I might not have skipped so gleefully to tell my mother that school was, in the phrase of the time, a lead-pipe cinch.

James Hearst

JAMES HEARST has been both a man of the land and a poet all his life, and you will find both those characteristics in this essay. He has also been a philosopher and teacher and you will find that side also. "Nothing is free except the time you have to live," he says at one point. "Change and weather wait on no one," he says at another.

In his seventy-six years, Hearst has produced only a half dozen slender books of poems but these are enough to stamp him as Iowa's major poet, which is an achievement in a state that has also produced Paul Engle and Arthur Davison Ficke. His old friend, Bill Reninger, once compared Hearst favorably to Robert Frost (whose name you will find in the pages that follow). The comparison, while good, is unnecessary—Jim Hearst can stand on his own record. I am grateful to have known him, and my life has been the better for having the opportunity to read his verse.

Little of Hearst's poetry is in this essay of 1976, though the prose has a rhythm and swing that only a poet could produce. What there is in God's plenty was what it was like to grow up on an Iowa farm in the first quarter of this century—and on a farm that should give the lie, if one is necessary, to New Yorkers' concepts of the Iowa farmer as a "hick" or "hayseed."

But enough. My words are only standing in the way. It's best that you get on to far better words—and be quick about it. You'll not be sorry.

YOUNG POET ON THE LAND

ON AN IOWA farm on August 8, 1900, the heat brought out the sweat early in the day on the threshers' faces. The work, the dust, the soft chuff-chuff of the big steam engine, the loud continuous hum of the separator as it knocked the oats out of the straw sheaves, fanned out the dust and chaff, funneled the grain into wagons. The machines cost the farmer three cents a bushel, but the help came from the neighbors. Each neighborhood composed a threshing ring—farmers who helped each other with the summer harvest. Today they gathered at the Hearst farm, operated by James Hearst's middle son Charles. A good day for threshing, hot, dry, no wind to speak of. The oats threshed easy on dry days.

The tune and rhythm of harvest spoke for the time. All gathering of grain and fruit composes its own music. This year at the Hearst farm an additional note sounded. Katherine Hearst (nee Schell), wife of Charles Hearst, sweat and struggled through the birth of her second child, a boy this time. The baby squalled his protest and wiggled in the doctor's hands. His cry did not drown out the voice of the machines outside. Perhaps it never would. Not a very large baby but active. He never outgrew the restlessness shown at his birth. But now he just wiggled and squalled and had no way of knowing he would be called James after his Grandfather Hearst and cared less. The birth not difficult but long, Katherine held the baby against her breast and they both slept.

The house almost new, for a house it could be called new. Built four years before, a two-story farmhouse with four bedrooms upstairs and a dining room, sitting room, parlor, and kitchen downstairs. What made it unusual was the arc of a porch around the front of the house, beautiful oak finish inside, and most unusual, a zinc-lined bathtub in a hall off the kitchen.

By the time I was able to walk and talk the porch had rambler roses climbing each pillar and on the west end a trellis supported a net of honeysuckle vines where the hummingbirds used to come. Mother stayed a flower raiser all her life. The duties of a farmwife never kept her from her sweet peas and nasturtiums and bleeding heart. It humbles me to this day how she ever managed to satisfy all the voices that called to her. Just her

household duties would discourage most women today. She raised four
children, three boys and a girl. She kept the house clean, fed her family
three meals a day and this often included two hired men. She used linen
tablecloths and napkins every day and never complained about the
amount of washing and ironing. I can remember how on a hot July
morning she would come downstairs and start heating the "sad irons," as
they were called, at 4 A.M. so that she might finish the ironing before the
greatest heat of the day. She ironed the sheets and pillowcases too and the
roller towels and handkerchiefs and starched Father's white shirts for
Sunday wear.

In the winter she washed out in the woodshed and hung the clothes
on the clothesline out-of-doors. Sometimes the sheets would freeze on the

*"We youngsters resented
the fact that our house stood
on the west side of the
crossroad . . ."*

THE HEARST FARMSTEAD IN WINTER.

line and had to be taken down with great care lest they crack. On bitterly
cold days the clothes hung in clouds of cloth around the red-eyed hard coal
burner and the wood-burning kitchen range. Folding clothes bars held
some of them, the backs of chairs and even the dining room table took
their share. We used to play hide-and-go-seek among the drying clothes.
The need to save kept her mending and darning under the kerosene lamp
most evenings, though she always found time to read aloud to us before
we went to bed. The fairy tales of the brothers Grimm and Hans An-
dersen, old folk tales, still echo in my ears. My brother Robert loved a story
called "The Robber Kitten" and he insisted on it being read each night,
and he wanted it read exactly the same way each time. Mother never
seemed to tire of repeating it. We acquired our love of reading, I think,

from her. No matter how little money we had, books came to us as birthday and Christmas presents, we always had books. Mother's sisters, Aunt Vol (Viola), Aunt Mary, Aunt Ida (an M.D.) sent us books. Later when we were older the magazines, *St. Nicholas* and *Youths' Companion,* appeared in our Christmas stockings. We all could read before we went to school.

Mother planted a large vegetable garden too, though Father helped with this, and as soon as we could handle a hoe and tell a bean sprout from a smartweed we found ourselves in the garden. Then in the spring the chickens claimed Mother's attention. Two incubators in the cellar—not a basement but a cellar with an earth floor—filled with eggs to be watched, turned, temperature checked, moisture regulated, the family backed off in their demands while the eggs waited to hatch. Mother raised purebred barred Plymouth Rock chickens and she took great care, in the roosters she bought, to keep the bloodlines matched. Then the chicken coops had to be scraped, washed, fumigated, sun dried before the baby chicks could be housed.

The chicks seemed to attract catastrophes. Everything about them turned into a crisis. Medicine added to the drinking water, droppings examined for signs of diarrhea, a watch kept on the sky lest their guardian angel go off duty and a sudden rainstorm drown half of them before we could whoosh them into shelter. Then crows and hawks threatened them. Once after I had become old enough to use a shotgun, I fired right through the kitchen window at one wise old crow. Mother rejoiced over the end of the crow, scolded me for a broken window. But crows inherit an ancient wisdom of self-protection. I have seen them molest a young jackrabbit all morning, trying to pick its eyes out, when I worked in a field. But after lunch when I hung the shotgun on the tractor fender, nary a crow, one glint off the gun barrel and they disappeared.

After the children grew old enough to go to school, Mother not only fixed breakfast for the family and hired help but packed four lunches for us to carry as we started at eight o'clock to trudge the mile and a half to country school. It amazes me to see mothers today pack their kids in a car and haul them a few blocks to school and come and pick them up in the afternoon. From the time we were six years old we walked a mile and a half to school and a mile and a half home. We ate a sturdy breakfast, eggs and bacon or ham, sometimes fried potatoes, sometimes pancakes, always milk and homemade bread, nearly always oatmeal with thick cream on it, and in the winter, prune sauce. But still the walk stretched out a long way for short legs. No reprieves either, it took a heavy rain or storm before Father would come to get us. One winter morning, the thermometer standing at ten below, a driving northwest wind to face, Louise and Bob and I formed a half circle and walked with our backs to the wind and protected, in the screen of our bodies, Chuck as he plowed along with his head down. He hated to give up, Chuck did, he being the youngest felt the bad weather the most, but he wouldn't admit he was licked. Time came when Mr. Bergstrom drove over for his children and we rode halfway home with them. My father's Scotch-Irish blood seemed to say, harden the children, let them learn what life is like. We learned all right.

The sandwiches froze in our lunch pail, especially the ones with jelly. We crouched around the big black stove in the middle of the schoolroom, among the mittens and overshoes placed there to dry, and ate our lunches brought in from the cloakrooms. Cloakroom? A bare room with a row of hooks. In one a water pail on a stand and a tin dipper, we all drank from that. Though before I graduated from the eighth grade we had a water cooler with a push-button faucet and we used paper cups. A new family moved into the neighborhood with a sick father, tuberculosis, and mothers insisted on a different arrangement for the drinking water. Men never seem to worry about things like this until after an accident happens.

We youngsters resented the fact that our house stood on the west side of the crossroad and we must go to the west school. We met the neighbors going to town in the morning, and we met them as they went home in the afternoon. No chance for a ride, we were always going the wrong way. Warm spring and fall days blessed us and we loitered home from school, often barefooted, cutting across meadows and pastures to spy a meadowlark's nest with its twisted roof of grass or clumps of shooting stars, which Louise took home to Mother. Once I caught a black snake, long, thin, muscular, and tried to crack its head off as I had seen the hired man do, and it wrapped around my neck and nearly strangled me. Later I learned that it belonged to the constrictor family of snakes.

Later we three boys found skis in our Christmas stockings and we skied cross-country to get to school. We could do the mile and a half in ten minutes. Sometimes, just for the hell of it, we would put a breast collar on one of the ponies and fasten the tugs to a six-foot wooden rod, one of us would ride the pony, the others hang on to the stick and off we went skijoring across the fields, the pony's hoofs throwing balls of snow in our faces. Once in a while if I had to come home at noon to help Father or if I had stayed at home in the morning to help sort pigs or shell corn, I rode the biggest pony to school and put her in Mads Madsen's barn. But Father frowned on this, none of the other kids had ponies and he didn't want us to seem stuck-up. He needn't have worried, nobody had much money in those days and we played one-old-cat and work-up as if the best man was the one who hit the ball the farthest. We played prisoner's base and anty-over too and sometimes the teacher played. I fell in love with all my women teachers.

When I started to school, the school year lasted only eight months, November always corn-husking vacation. The big boys came to school for the winter term, young men twenty years old, with watch chains hanging from their vest pockets. They scared me half to death with their casual ways. We were taught at home to respect authority. Imagine my horror one day when the big boys suddenly rose from their seats, opened a window, and tossed the teacher into a snow bank. The teacher, a man, came back wiping off the snow and slid an icicle down the neck of one of his persecutors. After a scuffle, everything settled down again.

We had double seats, I sat with Thorvald Nelson the first year and he protected me from the older boys. He must have been sixteen or eighteen at the time, a gentle, courteous young man. He never plagued the women teachers nor did any of the other big boys. They soon stopped coming to school and by the time I hit the eighth grade, we assumed a nine month school year.

I gradually climbed the ladder of seniority and by the time the eighth grade took me to its bosom, I was the "big boy." I was sent across the road for water for the water fountain and Mrs. Madsen invited me in to have a cup of coffee. She and I would sit at the kitchen table with our coffee while school went on without me. But the teacher never scolded me for dallying.

She was a lovely girl, this teacher, named Olga Lundell. Her beautiful auburn hair shone in the sunlight, and her soft pleasant voice held me in a trance. Three of us finished the eighth grade that year and she felt the obligation to prepare us for the county board examinations. If we passed them, the city high schools would accept us. Long before this I had read all the books in our scanty school library, had spent some time huddled over the dictionary looking for words like "whore," which I never found as I searched through the *h*s. I suppose she did not know what to do with me, so in an inspired moment she asked me to put into verse form the stories in our literature book. She called it poetry. She snagged me right there. For the rest of the school year I bent to my task and the dictionary with its cargo of hidden words whirled away into neglect.

I had matched words by sound almost from the time I could make my *s*s the wrong way as I printed the letters, chewing on my tongue. But never for the public gaze. Oh, I did show one poem to my mother, I don't remember that she seemed impressed. But Miss Lundell found my work praiseworthy and said so. So I sweated out rhymes with the intensity of a man of dedication and of it all I can remember two lines from a story called the "Black Brothers," which ran, "And to the poor dog he would not give a bone/So he was turned into a black stone." The eyes of Miss Lundell gazed on me with soft approval when I showed her my work. Do you wonder that I loved her?

That year sang the end of country school for me, of box socials, school programs, Christmas parties, visits from parents and the county superintendent. Once we made valentines on Valentine's Day. I made ten valentines and gave one to every girl in school from the first grade to the eighth grade. When the teacher who acted as the postman delivered the valentines there was none for me. This seemed a bit unfair to me but I took it philosophically until the teacher called attention to it. Then in spite of my manly indifference, a sob rose in my throat and tears came to my eyes. Years of experience have never taught me how to cover neglect with a show of indifference. Inside me a little boy tries to keep from crying because he received no valentines.

When our time came to graduate from country school we all attended the high school connected with Iowa State Teachers College. The college used it as a training ground for student teachers and in those days everyone called it the Training School. The college ran on the quarter system so every three months we faced a new set of teachers, senior students, young men and women who planned to make a career of teaching. This meant a

"Grandfather loved birds and animals. . . . His death shocked me, I didn't know that grandfathers died."

(LEFT TO RIGHT) COUSIN HELEN McALVIN; SISTER LOUISE; COUSIN JAMES McALVIN; AUTHOR; HIS FATHER, CHARLES; AND HIS GRANDFATHER, JAMES.

confrontation between inexperienced, sometimes timid, young teachers and students old in ways of testing the nerve and authority of the teacher. Once in a while a supervisor would be called in to set us in order, but mostly, after a few days of high jinks, we settled down to business. I remember one teacher of English who found me such an apt pupil that she gave me a 97 for my first month's grade. Of course I could not face the other boys with a grade like that, so the next month I behaved so badly that my grade was 74—sort of evened things out. (I discovered with pleasure in my college teaching that a young man could work for good grades without reproach from his peers.) In my senior year I became so fond of my geometry teacher that I took her on a few dates, though this violated the rules of the authorities.

The road from the farm to the high school measured three and a half miles. This meant transportation. The first year when she had no one to ride with, my sister Louise stayed with my aunt and uncle, the Frank Hammers, who lived just across from the campus. (She tested out of Latin and German and finished high school in three years.) The next year she and I drove back and forth with a horse and buggy. A half dozen of us, students from the country, kept our horses in the barn of a retired preacher for three dollars a month. All the country kids west and south of town went to the Training School. That explains the strong athletic teams we fielded. The last year my two younger brothers, Bob and Chuck, played on the football team, played everybody who would take them on and won most of the games. We lost to Cedar Rapids for the state championship but larruped our archrival, Cedar Falls High, 38 to 0.

Then Father bought us a used Model T Ford and our adventures with it sound like a chapter from the ''Wizard of Oz.'' Country roads in those days offered fields to conquer, either we shoved and ground our way through mudholes or shoveled our way through snowdrifts. The high school principal kept a stack of tardy slips all made out for us, we so often missed the opening bell. Our excuses may have sounded exaggerated to her but they were never far from the truth. She must have wondered that we arrived at all.

My mother insisted on Latin and German, much to my embarrassment, few boys went this road. But I graduated in three and a half years and enrolled in college courses my last year since my high school schedule required only one class. I found myself in the same college class with my student teacher in high school. We both kept this a secret from the other students, but I'm sure she wondered how it happened.

Chores on a farm, to quote America's favorite poet, Robert Frost, never stay done. I learned that early in life without any help from Robert Frost. I started by drying dishes while my sister washed them. Next I brought in wood from the wood house in a basket for the kitchen stove. Then I entered the chicken chores department where I fed and watered the chickens and hunted the eggs. Many a tussle I had with a setting hen that pecked me sharply on the hand if I attempted to reach under her for eggs. It hurt. I finally worked out a method of handling these broody sisters by throwing my cap over their heads and then quick as a wink jerking them from the nest by their tail feathers. I broke an egg or two on occasion but saved myself from harm. I can see them yet, the old biddies with ruffled feathers, clucking and scratching under my feet, eyeing the nest to which they would jump the minute my back was turned. Stupid, silly things, I thought, mean too—I've disliked chickens ever since.

But my graduation took place when I could go out with the men and help with the barn chores. On a farm boys grow up by trying to do men's work. This ambition forced me into the straitjacket of necessity, where duty bound me with stronger demands than ever the chicken chores had done. At first my pride stirred when at five in the morning my father woke me to jump on a horse and bring up the cows from the pasture where they grazed all night. My manhood praised me when I sat on the back steps with the hired man, laced up my shoes, and stumbled sleepily toward the barn. The time came when I hated the everlasting baskets to be filled with corn, the hay to be thrown down from the haymow, the swill barrel in the hog house to be emptied into the troughs and filled again. This was a boy's rebellion against the tyranny of routine work. Later I knew all the farm tasks belonged to the larger ebb and flow of growing crops and animals. It showed me the way I wanted to go.

Father never pushed us into any of the chores. But once we volunteered, even begged, to do a job and proved we could do it we were bound to it like a serf to his chief. My brother Bob went out to the barn with me. Though he was two years younger, he stood taller and weighed more than I did. And Bob had a secret skill and innate stubbornness to avoid work he disliked, although he never shirked a job once he was committed to it. This left Chuck to handle the chicken chores far longer than he would have wished, but Mother needed help and he filled the places Bob and I had left.

We urged Father to let us cultivate corn, and on the condition that Bob sit on the end of the tongue and drive the horses while I manipulated the handles to guide the shovels, we won our argument. Topsy and Dolly, the slowest team on the farm—I can see their broad fat rumps ambling down the corn rows. Bob, impatient and eager to show progress, tried yelling and line slapping to move the team along. A cob had been left in the toolbox to clean off the shovels, and at my suggestion Bob jammed it in Topsy's rear end. The effect was electric. Up the corn row we went at a gallop, Topsy alternately trying to push the cob out, and then because it hurt, clamping her tail down tight on it and driving it in again. On one of her jumps she kicked up her legs and her hock struck Bob on the side of the face and knocked him off the cultivator. The side of his face stayed swollen for days. Finally Topsy got rid of the cob, I stopped the team, and we all headed for home, leaving a row of plowed-up corn plants. No doubt we explained it but I don't remember the excuse we used. No doubt my father suspected shenanigans, he was a hard man to fool. All I remember is the sudden jerks and leaps made by the cultivator, my desperate efforts to control the shovels, the fountains of dirt spraying up mixed with green corn plants, and the yell of pain and surprise from brother Bob as he fell off the cultivator. We never tried to stimulate a slow horse in that way again.

Memories of hired girls and hired men run past in a film strip in my mind. Danes, most of them, just migrating from Denmark, called "greenhorns," with no words of English except among the men an occasional "goddam." Cedar Falls was called "little Denmark" in those days and boasted a Danish newspaper, the *Dannevirke,* with the largest circulation of any Danish newspaper in the country. My father learned to speak a little Danish and he could understand most of what the men said. Even I could "schnock a little Dansk," a great help at school where all the kids were Danes and spoke Danish if they did not want to play with us. I know how it feels to be in a minority group.

One of the hired girls, named Ida, used to corral us everyday after dinner for our naps. Fleet of foot and strong (she had worked out-of-doors in her home country), she picked us up by the collar and seat of our pants and shoved us upstairs to bed. Chuck, the minute his dinner was finished, took off like a frightened fawn to escape nap time. But he always hid in the same place and Ida always found him, snug in a corner on the north side of Grandfather's house.

Ida's temper fascinated us. One day she picked up the pan of potatoes she was peeling, opened the kitchen door, and threw the whole thing, pan and all, out into the woodshed. Mother, curious, asked her why she did it. And Ida said in her broken English, "Oh, Mrs. Hearst, I just get so mad, so mad, I have to do something." Then she went out in the woodshed, picked up the potatoes, peeled them, and all was clear sailing again. We hung around Ida a lot, watching for these outbursts of temper. She once put a goose in the oven with all the entrails still in it. She had decided not to go to church, so before we went Mother asked her if she knew how to roast a goose. "Ja, ja," Ida said. But then she said "Ja, ja" to most things. We ate macaroni and cheese for dinner that Sunday. Ida married one of our hired men, Hans Thompsen, who played the accordion so beautifully that even Carlo the dog howled his appreciation.

We had a hired man who became a member of our family. Lauritz Nielsen, former coachman for the king of Denmark, came to America to seek his fortune. Mr. Holst, publisher of the *Dannevirke,* who served as a counsel for many of the Danish emigrants, sent him out to our farm. We adored Lauritz. He went to church with us, to all our picnics and family holiday dinners. We exchanged Christmas presents—once he gave me a real leather riding whip with a leather loop at the handle. He taught me the lessons of horse care. A strict taskmaster, he taught me how to handle colts, how to adjust the bit in a bridle, how to trim forelock, mane, and tail. I saw him and my father shoe horses but I never tackled that. He taught me to use the kind word and firm hand, how to sit in a saddle like a man not some hobbledehoy. By the time I was sixteen I was breaking our colts to the harness and plow all because Lauritz had taught me secrets from the great book of the Horse.

One Fourth of July when we could not wake up our parents so that we could go out and shoot off our firecrackers, Lauritz took the twelve-gauge shotgun and fired it off twice under the parents' bedroom window. No wonder we loved him. Mother would go out to a luncheon and leave us in Lauritz's care. He prepared our dinner and made us say a grace before we ate. We were not allowed to drink coffee. But Lauritz set out coffee cups for us all, diluted the coffee, and gave us each a cupful. Then he shook his finger and solemnly warned us, "Don't tell your mother or she give you some good spanking." But Chuck was too young to keep secrets and the minute Mother drove in the yard, Chuck ran out and excitedly asked her, "Do you know what we had for dinner?" Then it all came out and Mother pointed her finger at Lauritz and he hung his head in mock dismay.

Father loved picnics and family dinners. Our family, Father's family, mostly had settled in this vicinity, and we could count on about thirty members at a gathering, counting Grandfather and Grandmother, aunts, uncles, cousins, and a few distant connections. A place up the river called Kelley's Woods became our rendezvous for picnics. By carriage, buggy, spring wagon, and sometimes horseback we would congregate there for a Fourth of July picnic. Just the spot for a picnic, an open glade of long grass surrounded by trees growing back a mile to the road, the river flowing past at our feet. Those tremendous picnic dinners with fried chicken and watermelon—real fried chicken, not skinny pieces buried in stale batter but big husky birds that put on muscle walking about in the chicken yard, whose leg and thigh looked as big as that of a yearling steer to us kids.

Two of my uncles, doctors, insisted that we children wait an hour after we had stuffed ourselves with food before we put on our bathing suits and took to the water. Nearly everyone went swimming, men, women, and children. A long sandbar enclosing shallow water made a safe pool for the little kids. In those days if you cut your foot, it would be on a clam shell, not a beer can.

Father, the second son in a family of seven, chose to stay on the farm. I never knew what arrangement he had with Grandfather. Grandfather Hearst lost interest in the operations of a 320-acre farm and let my father run the place. Grandfather was a bee and orchard man. I felt proud when he took me by the hand and showed me how to graft new varieties of apples on old trees or how to remove a full super of honey and replace it with an empty (though here I stood back a respectable distance, bees and I were strangers to each other).

We kept up the orchard for years after Grandfather died. What a harvest of apples, barrel after barrel filled to the top. The corncrib where they found temporary storage smelled so good I used to go in just to sniff the air. Once, walking through the orchard with my father, a young man then, I pointed out a tree with a great knot in the trunk and asked what could have happened to it. He sort of grinned and said, "One day when I had been a naughty youngster, Father sent me out to cut a switch to punish me with. He had just planted some prize apple trees—he called them whips—he had imported from Ohio. To revenge myself for the licking I was about to get, I grabbed one of these slender whips and tied a knot in it. Father didn't dare untie it for fear of breaking the wood, so he left it and it grew all right but always had this deformity."

Then we went on but it pleased me in some boyish way to know that Father had not always been the model of rectitude we thought him. No, I shouldn't say that, for whatever rebellious and independent spirit works in me came from my father as well as my mother. It was all very well for Grandfather to read "Snowbound" to us each winter, cozy in front of the fire, eating apples and popcorn while the wind blew and snow fell outside. But what about the shot heard 'round the world that the farmers fired at Concord? And Tom Payne's "summer soldier"? And Thoreau's marching to a different tune? This spirit stayed alive deep beneath Father's pleasant and friendly manner. My father belonged to the group of farm leaders named by Senator Moses of New Hampshire, as "sons of wild jackasses." He labored mightily with such mavericks as Senator Smith W. Brookhart and Senator Robert La Follette to persuade Congress to pass legislation to help the farmer. We met men like these in our living room on many a Sunday afternoon.

My father knew farming and purebred Shorthorn cattle but was ignorant and innocent in the ways of the business world. In my files still is a certificate for one hundred shares of an oil company formed to drill for oil around Cedar Falls, where the only oil ever found filled 3-in-1 cans and kerosene lamps. But he had bad luck with his boys. My brother Robert, a strong, well-built young man, a terror as tackle on the football team, died at the age of 23 of lymphatic sarcoma. Death came at the end of two costly years of hospitals and treatments. And I mistook the depth of water as I dove off a boat dock and spent the next two years in the hospital. These expenses and worries and anxieties piled on top of sharply declining farm prices and mortgage foreclosures while we stayed "cool with Coolidge."

Our family attended church regularly if not devoutly. We lost the habit when my brother Bob fell sick and never picked it up again. But at one time, every Sunday the Hearst family marched into church (a little

"Father loved picnics and family dinners."

THANKSGIVING, 1935. COUNTERCLOCKWISE FROM FATHER (BACK TO CAMERA),
CHARLES, GUEST, LOUISE, MOTHER, JAMES, AND GUESTS.

late, it took an hour to drive to town) with clean necks and ears and shined
shoes and settled down in the family pew. Grandfather and Grandmother
belonged to the Scotch-Presbyterian faith, and as a boy, it seemed to me
the worst religion in the world. The Sunday was the Sabbath and on the
Sabbath one did not run and play, nor whistle and shout, nor throw a ball,
nor even have a fire in the cookstove. But they settled for the
Congregational church in Cedar Falls. It seems disloyal to say it, but when
Grandfather died, Sunday lost its threat of hairshirts and sackcloth.

Grandfather wore no gloom, he seemed cheerful and friendly with
me, his namesake. But his impatience and restless spirit kept him on the
move and critical of slower moving folk. And Grandmother, unhurried
and gracious, with a pleasant expression and Down-East accent, kept him
in check. She said, "If dinner isn't ready when James comes champing at
the bit, I just set the table. When he sees the knives, forks, and napkins all
laid out, he sits down and reads the paper, sure that dinner is almost
ready." Grandfather loved birds and animals, he had a pet crow that
talked, a pair of pet squirrels that used to hide in the parlor curtains and

leap out on the unsuspecting guest. The only time he laid hands on me in anger he shook me until my teeth rattled because I shot at one of his cherished martins with my slingshot. He taught me many of nature's secrets as I trotted after him to orchard and beehive. His death shocked me, I didn't know that grandfathers died. I missed holding his hand, I was only seven.

The close of World War I tore off the leaves of all previous calendars. The dirt country road ended in a closed sign, and the new pavement pointed in another direction. In the barn the horse stalls emptied, we traded in our last team of horses on a new combine, the first one in our neighborhood. No more threshing rings, country school programs (buses took the schoolchildren to town schools), no more barn dances, sharing the work, silo filling, shredding, building. When our house burned on a July day, neighbors left their fields and carried out beds and chairs before the fire department could get there. To a degree the sociability and neighborly inquiry disappeared. The machine shed sheltered tractors and the big plows and heavy disks, even wagons ran on rubber tires. Oil and gasoline fed the iron horses, baled hay was ground for cattle and hog feed or sold. The hay-loader and corn binder melted away under the hands of rust and weather back of the trees on the junk pile.

Farming had been called a way of life but now it became a business. Farmers began to record their gains and losses. It mattered how many pounds of feed a steer ate, how many months it took to bring a pig to market weight, the milk production of dairy cows, the amount of gas and oil to plow a thirty-acre field. Bankers stopped telling their farm customers to stay at home and tend to their business. This was the conventional reply of town businessmen to farmers who complained of the sinking farm prices. But now the president of the bank met farm customers with a handshake, and loans and mortgage extensions helped ease relationships between them. The government stepped in with Production Credit loans and Federal Land banks and the local banks suddenly woke up and pressed for business.

The way back through the plowed fields and tree stumps of memory, mounted on a slow horse, takes me up one path and down another. The urgent and pressing push of the generative spirit we took for granted. The whole farm stirred and sweated in an effort to create a new multitude. Shelled corn grew moist and warm in the bin when planting time came and many a farmer found himself with bushels of moldy corn if he failed to take this into account. Everything came into blossom, weeds, flowers, trees, and we picked the pussy willow as the first spring sign.

We watched the rooster run down the hen and for a long time I believed that he spit the sperm in the top of the hen's head when he grabbed her. My sex education wrote itself out in all kinds of actions. My father, in an effort to give me a lesson in the reproductive process, asked me if I knew how a calf was born. And to fox him, because even at five years old I knew better, I said it came out of the cow's side. Father looked at me sharply and ended the lesson. Once on a day when my cousin was coming to visit Father asked me how many bad words I knew. I had gone to the field with him, he was sitting on the corn planter ready to start planting. A warm sunny May day, too young still to be in school, I leaned against the planter wheel and told him. I can see him yet take off his hat and wipe his forehead as he said, "I guess that's all of them." Here I lived isolated in the country, not yet in school, yet with a full knowledge of all the "bad words." No wonder to this day I regard with skepticism anyone's attempt to set up as censor to "protect the children."

We saw the boar breed the sows and the bull mount the cows, probably with curiosity at first, but soon we accepted it as a familiar and routine sight. The one thing that intrigued us was the visit each week of the stud horse man. Usually late in the afternoon he came trailing up the road, driving a tired-looking, scrawny-necked mare hitched to a two-wheeled cart and leading a huge magnificent stallion. His picture and pedigree nailed to the inside wall of the horse barn told us what an important Belgian stallion he was and gave his name, Parthos de Sarlongdingue. We kids, a little scared and bug eyed, marveled at his great arched neck, his blue coat of hair, legs like fence posts, muscles bulging as he pranced, shoulders and rump massive—we said among ourselves that his ass spread out like the haymow door. But even he could have come and gone without much interest after we grew used to him except for one thing.

Poor Father, in an effort to protect the innocence of his young children, gave the order for all of us to go to the house and stay there when a mare needed to be bred. Two of my cousins, Helen and James McAlvin, lived with us then, Jim my age and Helen the age of my sister Louise. That made six of us. The performance took place back of the big barn, at the west end, away from the house and the road. A low shed up to the barn at right angles and a granary on the other side made the west end of the barn a secluded spot. When the mare had been bred, Lauritz, who was holding her halter rope, said to my father, "Charlie, look!" and he pointed. And there peeking over the ridge pole of the shed shone four interested pairs of eyes. We climbed up the shed roof, my brothers Bob and Chuck, Jim McAlvin, and I. And hid under the granary, heads sticking out around the stones of its foundations, were Louise and Helen. It was the lure of the forbidden, I'm sure, that brought us there, though there is a kind of wonder and excitement when horses mate.

When I was about ten years old, Father bought a small Arabian mare for us to ride and drive. Think of it, a horse of our own, a new western-type saddle and bridle to boot. She had been bred to a Shetland pony stallion and gave birth to a little mare colt not much larger than a big dog.

We couldn't take our eyes off this wonderful plaything. We called her Trix and she lived up to her name. She shook hands, walked on her hind legs, walked up the wood house stairs—startled my mother almost out of her wits one day when she met Trix unannounced on the platform by the kitchen door. But her knack of opening barn doors and feedlot gates at last deprived her of liberty. After my father found the cows nosing through the garden, the horses from the pasture tearing around the yard, his patience came to an end. "You kids," he ordered, "keep that fool pony tied up from now on. No more running around loose. Those horses get out in the cornfield and a belly full of green corn and we'd have some sick horses on our hands. Now tie her up!"

The Johnny Call farm between Cedar Falls and Waterloo once raised ponies for circuses and traveling shows. When Mr. Call died, his son George sold off all the ponies except the stallion, a feisty Shetland named King. We took our mare over there to be bred. One day he said, "Why don't you take the stud home with you? Keep him all summer, hell, keep him all year if you want to, I've no use for him and I kind of hate to sell him."

So King came to live in our barn and we bred our mares to him. We bred the Arabian, and as soon as she was old enough, we bred Trix. They both had mare colts. You can see what happened. By the time I was a senior in high school, we had a dozen ponies around the place. By this time we had almost outgrown them.

We *had* outgrown them. Father insisted that they were our responsibility and even when they ran in the pasture we had to trim their manes and tails and trim their hoofs. It was too much, our interests lay elsewhere. High school with its new friends, basketball, parties, and the pressure of more regular study habits demanded our attention and the ponies lost out. One day Father sold the whole caboodle to the Clyde Miller circus and savages that we are, we never wept a tear. Let them go, we had other chores to do.

None of us will forget our fishing trips to the creek a mile and a half away. With our homemade fish poles—Chuck even ~~concocted~~ FASHIONED a reel from a big spool and nailed it to his pole. Then with Trix hitched to the coaster wagon by a flimsy singletree at the end of the tongue, four of us crowded on the wagon and tore down the road as fast as Trix could gallop. My cousin usually sat at the back because he was older and when he fell off he didn't get hurt. Not much room for four boys on a coaster wagon. I drove and most of the time I could not see the road through the cloud of dirt and gravel flying from Trix's hind feet. But we got there and back and caught our minnows, which Mother—bless her heart—fried for us for supper. No one broke an arm or leg though some of the neighbors complained to my father that "those kids will kill themselves."

We played pony polo too, with long willow sticks stuck in the heads of croquet mallets. Two to a side, we banged the croquet ball, ourselves, and the ponies' heads. The ponies learned to run with their heads down to protect themselves from the swinging mallets. We rode bareback, so of course we fell off every time we reached over to take a swipe at the ball.

Now it seems innocent and carefree, the life we led, but it was not. The struggle to make a farm pay its way had begun. In my grandfather's day, the farm took care of itself—the windmill pumped the water, the woodlot furnished the fuel, logs from the sawmill provided the material for repairs, taxes were light, the land increased in value every year. But history turned a page and my father tried to make the farm meet his money needs, to pay off the brothers and sisters their share in the farm, to pay for new and more expensive machinery, better clothes for his wife and children, increased taxes, and the demands for better roads, better teachers, the flow of commodities from town to farm, from farm to market. A slow and difficult change from an old path to a new road. The horse buyer from town and the price of hogs suddenly became important. We children did not know it but we felt a sharper edge to the wind.

My childhood days should have been happy ones. My parents, kind and protective, two brothers and a sister to play with, we were a close-knit family. But I found myself moody, irritable, stubborn, resentful of words of correction, of my share of the chores. Sometimes I knew I had been adopted and made to do the hardest work of anyone. Dreamy and quick to learn, I loved a corner where I sat hidden with a book and no one knew I was there. My folks had a set of Scott's novels and when I became old enough to read them, I found my nirvana. I can still hear my father coming into the house and asking, "Where's that boy?" I wore a sullen face when pulled out of my reverie into a world where chickens must be fed, wood baskets filled, eggs gathered. Because I was the eldest boy, more responsibility came my way than to my brothers. "Remember James, you are the oldest, watch out for your brothers." I loved my brothers but this added burden frustrated me and made me angry. I had to pull my punches in competitive play, which soured my enjoyment over a visit to my cousin in Waterloo. My conscience always played the devil with me, I did not dare shirk responsibility. My brothers must have hated me many times for my rough bossy ways. But I knew what my parents expected of me and I dared not fail. No, I was not a happy child and to this day I taste the black bile of cynicism when folk go into raptures over the joys of childhood. Children walk the plank of experience barefooted and the splinters hurt them and cause them deep wounds beyond most adults' imagining.

The introduction of new seeds marked a milestone in farm progress. We raised Reid's Yellow Dent corn and picked out the good ears for seed as we husked the corn. Every wagon had a special box on it for these ears. (I won a silver cup in a corn judging contest at the fair.) We raised Silver King, a white corn, so that the southern whites could have white corn meal and not have to eat yellow corn. A red ear on a load of white corn stood out like a flame. (The trouble was there were no girls around to kiss.) The corn went down badly in a wind and made a jungle of broken stalks. Once Nels Madsen, driving our corn binder, at the end of a 120-rod field found himself six rows off from the row he started with, it was that tangled. Besides the great jump in yield, what a relief to have the stiff hybrid stalks that would stand up in the row until March.

Father made fun of our first hybrid corn—we bought the seed from Henry Wallace—with its long, limp ears, you could almost tie a knot in them. But when he saw the stalks still standing straight in December, he changed his tune. It had been a wet fall and we were still husking corn in December. As we expected, the neighbors needled us for planting corn with those funny-looking ears—not just our neighbors but the human race is suspicious of anything different—but not many years passed before no open pollinated corn was planted. The superiority of hybrid seed corn left the opposition no arguments.

Signs of boyhood linger in many corners of memory. Every time I pass the grove my grandfather planted with maple seeds he carried from Ohio I find them. The grove still stretches forty rods wide and about twenty rods deep, to boys it loomed up dark and mysterious as a forest. We pitched a wigwam there made of maple poles covered with horse blankets. In true Indian fashion we baked potatoes and sweet corn in the open fire and ate them half raw because we couldn't wait any longer. Our bows and arrows became dangerous weapons with tenpenny nails wired in for arrow heads and turkey feathers glued along the base. I shot an old sow once who had escaped from her pen and the arrow stuck in her ham as she ran squealing in full flight. My father pulled out the arrow and gave it to me without a word, but I got the message. We played Robin Hood in that grove and rode out of Ivanhoe with wooden swords and barrelhead shields that we whacked until one of us got hurt. The dark middle of the grove held all sorts of suspicions that we half feared might suddenly come to life.

But the grove played a less spooky part when, in March, we tapped the trees and gathered bucket after bucket of sap. We bored holes in the trees and drove in homemade wooden spiles and collected the sap in washed-out lard pails. My poor mother had the copper washboiler on the stove for days as we boiled down the sap to a few jars of syrup mixed with twigs and dead leaves. Poor Mother, stove covered with the boiler and the kitchen full of steam. Even my sister took part in this syrup-making process and helped us carry home the pails of sap. How patient Mother must have been with four lively children full of projects and the will to carry them out. I hope she enjoyed the excitement we found in life on a farm. I asked my mother once if she thought I would ever be able to earn one thousand dollars. And she said that she could tell better after I filled the wood basket. In my reading I ran across the term ''white slave'' (in a Sunday

School paper of all places) and I asked my mother what it meant. She said it meant "a woman used for immoral purposes." But I thought she said "immortal purposes" and I looked up immortal in the dictionary and it didn't seem like such a bad life.

We had any number of pets besides the familiar dogs and cats. We found young crows that had fallen out of the nest and we brought them home, confined them in a big box with screen over one side, and fed them bread soaked in milk. We caught little rabbits and fed them with an eyedropper. Once Chuck brought home a tiny civet cat that he found, wet, shivering, and deserted in the field. Just a small black ball with white dots, he slept on his nose with his tail curled over him, you could hold him in the palm of your hand. We named him "Carl Weeks" after the perfume manufacturer in Des Moines. He cuddled up in our hands or played

". . . two brothers and a sister to play with, we were a close-knit family."

(LEFT TO RIGHT) ROBERT; JAMES, AGE SEVEN; LOUISE; AND CHARLES.

with a string like a kitten. He lived with us, apparently happy, for some time until our veterinarian cautioned us that he might use his artillery on strangers, friends who came to visit us. Dr. Moles said that civet cats are born already charged and loaded and for us to watch out. We asked him to deodorize our friend and he said, "Not on your life." So, regretfully, Carl Weeks went back to the field where he was born. He was about three-quarters grown by then and we hoped he could cope with the exigencies of wild life. Apparently he did for we never saw or heard from him again.

We lived in the sweat and splendor of our own domain, untouched except for church and business by the indulgent ways of the town's cloven footed. Our innocence was not carefree. We felt bogged down in a swamp of duties. A price had to be paid for self-sufficiency. Chickens to care for, cream to be churned, garden crops harvested (all the canning and drying and packing in wet sand), butchering in the fall, which meant trying out the lard and smoking hams and bacon. It irritated us, no, we resented the ingenuity of adults for finding chores and tasks for children to do. We learned firsthand that healthy appetites no longer feed on manna from heaven but on food prepared by hardworking hands. This lesson stayed with me when I grew up—nothing is free except the time you have to live. It is a good thing to know and taught me many times how to make do with what I had.

How swiftly change rushes past. Farmers no longer keep chickens, milk a few cows, churn butter, butcher for their meat, tend a big vegetable garden. My mother baked 1200 pounds of flour a year into bread, biscuits, and cinnamon rolls. What farm wife now must bake her own bread? In order to play basketball I walked home three and a half miles on winter evenings, my hair, wet from the shower, frozen in a crown of ice. What farm family today does not have two vehicles at hand for use? My brothers drove the car home to help with the chores but I was glad to have the chance to play basketball and gladly I walked. Soon horses and all their needs and equipment vanished like smoke in the fire of the machine age. Now at the farm an electric wire substitutes for boy power, woman power, man power, and horse power. If that wire breaks the emergency is a critical one, no light, no heat, and worst of all, no water—once after an ice storm the fire department brought out a tank of water for the livestock.

Change and weather wait on no one. The momentum of our beginnings pushes us into our future. The early days of a boy on an Iowa farm, like seeds, contain the pattern of what will come. The party line, mud road, country school wrote their service in indelible ink, part of a record kept of barns cleaned, manure hauled, corn husked, labor by shovel and fork, the hard handwork of the time. They lie in the earth of my past, the earth where we all plant the seeds we hope to harvest.

But we welcomed the machine age with open arms. Engine power instead of muscle power, larger farms, private telephones, balanced account books, asphalt roads, bathrooms, promises of a better, at least easier, life. This is another layer added to the stratified terrain of a man's life.

In my books I have tried always to be aware that the earth, seed, and weather plus human skill and knowledge are the true roots of creation. Centuries do not change them even though, as Thomas Hardy said, "Dynasties fall." Today I look at my farm life and see what it meant in terms of endurance, courage, compassion, and struggle. The people I knew, our neighbors, had their share of clear skies and early frosts, of joy, grief, kindness, and loss. The poems try to say this. Poetry should not cheat. If truly written by the driven spirit it will not fail to show how goes the battle through revelation and insight.

I want my books to smell of the earth, of its sweat, dew, and sap, to expose its stillborn and stunted bodies, to praise its rich seasons. I want the poems to remember how it went to tell time by the sun, wind direction by a finger, coming storm by a restless herd. I speak only from the ground I stand on and for its people and their fields. I have tried to speak as honestly as I could with full knowledge that the earth will have the last word.

Paul Engle

PAUL ENGLE has been a lifelong resident of his native state, unlike most of his contemporaries who grew up in Iowa and then fled to more exotic climes—California, Chicago, Connecticut, New Mexico, Tahiti, or Florida.

He was born of German ancestry in Cedar Rapids and educated at old Washington High School and at Coe College. He holds the M.A. degree from the University of Iowa; his thesis, a collection of poems, was published as *Worn Earth* (1932) in the Yale Series of Younger Poets. He has since published a score of volumes of verse.

After a Rhodes scholarship at Merton College, Oxford, he came to Iowa City in 1937. With Wilbur Schramm, he edited the magazine *American Prefaces* and established the Writers' Workshop; he served as its director from 1941 to 1964. Then, with his second wife, Hua Ling Nieh, he founded the International Writers' Workshop. Engle retired from the university in 1977.

Among his nonpoetical works are a novel, *Always the Land* (1941), which reflects his farm background and his love for horses, and two books about Christmas in Iowa, *Prairie Christmas* (1960) and *An Old Fashioned Christmas* (1964), from which "Newsboy's Christmas" is taken. These two books are not only about Christmas but also about growing up in Iowa in the teens.

Engle, like James Hearst, has a delightful prose style. I am sure there are other Iowans who heartily endorse my wish that both these men had written more prose pieces in addition to their poetry.

NEWSBOY'S CHRISTMAS

AS A CARRIER boy who delivered newspapers to a hundred families along a route of two miles, I probably knew more about the progress of Christmas each year than anyone else. Ministers of the Gospel, businessmen, housewives, all had their individual efforts to make for the holiday, but I alone had the total view.

After school I walked to the Cedar Rapids *Gazette* to wait with the other boys in a large room in the basement. This was heated by the furnaces where lead cylinders from other editions were melted down.

There was usually time to kill, so I read the paper and noted the Christmas news and the advertisements for gifts. That way, I kept informed of all the events and activities which were coming.

Then we lined up and received the papers, and as I put my canvas bag over my left shoulder (so that the right arm would be free for throwing papers onto porches), the depressing increase in thickness and weight told me that the cheerful season was approaching.

By the week before Christmas my shoulder would be pulled down by the heaviness of all that wood pulp given over to the news and business of those last days. There were afternoons when I would stagger with the load if I had to walk through snow or over ice, until the first few dozen papers had been thrown with a fine holiday thud onto the porches.

The day after Christmas the papers would be so thin that the bag would seem to have no weight at all. That lightness meant another year to wait.

Trudging across the business district to the beginning of my route, I passed the big store windows, and could tell by the changes in them that the holiday was near, and what sort of things were offered each year. This also meant that I walked under the street decorations which the city put up, so that I began my long hike by passing under arches of colored lights and pine boughs. *That* is the way for a boy to start out on his little job every day!

My route itself was a clear indication of the Christmas excitement. On some day two or three weeks ahead I would look up the long street where I began my delivery of the world's glories and disasters. Streets were not as brightly illuminated in those days, so that any new radiance would stand out conspicuously. And there, shining out of a window onto the reflecting snow, the light wavering because it came from flickering candles and not electric bulbs, would be the first Christmas tree of the year. It shone there like a star which came to rest on Earth instead of moving through the restless sky.

St. Matthew says: "And lo, the star, which they saw in the east, went before them, till it came and stood over where the young child was. When they saw the star, they rejoiced with exceeding great joy."

When I saw that tree, I rejoiced with exceeding great joy, for I knew the Day above all other days was close at hand. My bag of papers seemed lighter, and I knew that each time I walked up that street, laid out in the unique American manner, a mile straight before it curved, there would be more trees shining out into the cold, gay air.

By Christmas Eve, there was hardly a house in which I could not see the pine or spruce or fir bright in a room, and as I carried that same route for several years, I came to know which houses were first to put up a tree, which always had a huge one from floor to ceiling, and which had a tiny one on a table.

There was another thing I came to know along that length of houses: the people who lived there. I knew which houses had old men who dug around the yard in May, and would give me cuttings of roses and wax begonias to put in my bag and take home to start in our own yard.

More than that, I knew which houses had people who always gave the boy a token on Christmas Eve.

There were families which had their tree in a room shut off from the rest of the house until Christmas morning, and there were a few which, sadly, never put up a tree at all. But no matter what they did in advance of the Day, I distinguished the houses quite selfishly in terms of those which always had a gift for me, and those which did not.

One thing I discovered—the houses which began decorating early, with a wreath at door and window and a tree large and gaily hung with ornaments, were most likely to remember the paper boy.

For days ahead I began warming up my customers by making certain they thought of me. I would throw the paper up against the door with a brisk bang. This became easier to do as the editions became heavier, so that close to Christmas my route became a succession of formidable thuds as the thick papers struck door and porch.

Toward the end of the route, which went up to the last houses at the edge of the city, people would hear the paper and invite me in to get warm. My oldest customers knew that I had a long walk home, and understood that the trudge out from the center of town to the edge would chill any boy.

In somewhat the same way that hoboes are supposed to mark houses

Ladies' Home Journal, 1913

*"By Christmas Eve, there was hardly a house in which I
could not see the pine or spruce or fir bright in a room. . . ."*

where they will get a generous reception, I had a precise knowledge of the places where I could expect a Christmas gift, all of the way out Fourth Avenue Southeast, to the city limits.

There was the last survivor of the Charge of the Light Brigade, a venerable Englishman who in summer gave me roses from plants he had brought from England. It was hard to imagine him as a young trooper riding into immortality on a fine bay horse, this quiet man digging in the black dirt which was such a wonder to him. But he had the saber and insignia to prove it.

He would wait for me on Christmas Eve, and I had orders to stop and knock. Inside, he would give me a fruitcake smelling richly of wine, and a half-dollar inside it. Standing there erect but gentle, and homesick for the green shire he would never see again, he would say, "Here, boy, real English cake, good for you in the winter."

The gifts would start quite close to the beginning of the route, so that as I went along throwing papers up to the doors, my bag would empty of the solid newspapers but I would replace them with little packages of gifts.

It was a comfort to me that the first gifts of all which I received were not from my own family, but from the people whom I was paid to serve. I was careful in throwing the paper on the porch on warm evenings not to

PAUL ENGLE, AGE FOUR, AND HIS SISTER ALICE; 1602 FIFTH AVENUE, CEDAR RAPIDS.

hit the baby playing in its pen, to break no windows, not to leave the paper on the roof or under bushes.

They were glad to have me bring the daily record of what seemed worth praise or fear or shame or anger in the country and in the world. And I was glad to have a modest recognition once a year of their kind thought of me. It was a cheerful relationship, and gave me a much more sympathetic view of life than later years would allow.

An ironic and skeptical attitude toward experience is often right and fine, but there is a wisdom in kindness, too. I was lucky to discover that young, carrying newspapers on Christmas Eve.

🌼 🌼 Frederick Manfred

"WINTER COUNT," from the book of the same title (1966), is unusual in this collection in at least one respect—it is a lengthy, rambling, unrhymed narrative poem. Although this poem appears in an anthology of poems by the same writer, its author is far better known as a novelist, short story writer, and book reviewer. He is also, on occasion, a teacher of writing.

As the poem tells us, Frederick Manfred was born at Doon, Iowa, in 1912 in Lyon County, southwest of Rock Rapids, the county seat. Doon was named nostalgically by its English settlers, but Manfred is the son of Frisian parents and descended (a fact he is proud to relate) from Frisian ancestors.

He has always been a writer; he has produced twenty-two novels and a number of shorter pieces in his career. He is certainly the tallest writer represented herein, a giant of a man at six feet nine inches. Among Iowa writers, he is a giant in quality as well as quantity.

Most of Manfred's work is set in the literary country he named: Siouxland. Siouxland includes far northwest Iowa, southwest Minnesota, southeast South Dakota, and northeast Nebraska. His works range through the history of Siouxland, from before the coming of the white man until the recent present. Like parts of this poem, his work is often earthy. Like parts of this poem, his work deals with birth and death and with the relationships among people.

WINTER COUNT

THE WINTER MORNING when I was born
a snowbank as big as a mountain
swept level with the eaves of the house.
Pa had to clip the barbwire fence
and cross the fields in his bobsled
to get the doctor from Doon.
The doctor came after I was born.
He told Gramma she made a good midwife.
Pa thought I was a champ,
and wanted to give me some beer,
which the doctor took instead.
Gramma, consulting her memories, said
she was afraid I took after both my grandfathers.
Gramma didn't like them much. They were giants.
Ma, smiling, gave her firstborn some titty.

The next cold winter Ma became heavy with Ed
and she dragged through the days
until he was born in July.
One look, and she knew she would
have to favor him for the rest of her life.

The next cold winter Ma said No to Pa.
So when sultry summer came along
she had it a little easier,
until one day I wandered off with Rover
and got lost in a cornfield.
A posse found me the second day.
My cheeks were sticky with corn milk.
There were traces of rabbit fur
along the purple edges of Rover's mouth.

The summer after the next winter
Ma asked me to watch over Ed,

be an older brother to him.
It was my job to keep Ed out of the kitchen
where Ma and Aunt Jenny were making plum preserve.
But the minute I left off watching
Ed would scoot past me and get into the plum pits.
This was bad for his intesteens, Aunt Jenny said.
Ed surely liked to suck them plum pits.
It was really Ma's fault though.
She'd let him be a tittyboy too long.

The next winter Ed and I were playing in the kitchen
while Ma was mopping the floor before supper.
Ma told me to keep Ed off the chairs
so he couldn't climb on the table where the butter was.
If you didn't watch him
Ed would sneak a finger of butter on you
and then go sit in a corner and lick it.
One time Ed got on the chair ahead of me.
I had to butt him to get him off.
Ed fell backwards into the mop pan
just as Ma was pouring in some fresh hot water.
Ed didn't even cry.
But Ma, she screamed, and then
quick emptied a box of baking powder down his back
in between his shirt and his skin.
She called Pa from his milking.
Pa was going go lick me,
but Ma wouldn't let him.
She said it really was her fault.
The burning water left a big red welt
across Ed's left shoulderblade.
Later, Ed got infantile paralysis
in his left arm and left leg.
Again Ma said it really was her fault.

One night late the next winter
I heard Ma yelling her head off.
Ed and I were sleeping together
in the southwest corner of the bedroom
so I couldn't help but hear all the yelling.
I peeked open my eyes and looked around.
The reflector on the yellow kerosene lamp
was shining straight at Ma's bed.
Pa and Doc Chalmers were talking in a corner.

Pretty soon Pa came over with a funny smile.
I quick closed my eyes and pretended to be asleep.
I heard Pa say, ''They never heard a thing.
They're both dead to the world.''
I don't know if Ed heard the yelling or not.
He was pretty sly too sometimes.
The next morning Pa told me some old news.
''You've got a brand new baby brother named Floyd,''
    he said.
I asked Pa if this new baby could talk.
''Why no, son. What makes you ask?''
''Well, if he can't talk
    how do you know his name is Floyd?''

''We hayed and shocked and picked corn together.''

STANDING IN REAR, LEFT TO RIGHT, GRANDFATHER, FREDERICK, AND FATHER.

That same fall I started school.
Pa brought me in the grinding Overland.
A lot of wild kids were running around.
Pa took me in to meet the teacher.
The teacher was nice. She smiled
to win me over like Ma always did.
"Don't you want to go out and play
    with all of your nice new friends?"
She put her hand on top of my head
and took me out on the front steps.
Pretty soon a friendly Berg girl came running up.
"Can he play pump-pump-pull-away, teacher?"
"Sure he can. Go ahead and play, Freddie."
That winter everything went along all right.
I walked the mile and a half to school
with the neighbor Berg kids.
Snowstorms didn't bother us much.
I had a blue stocking cap
and some good red boots.
Once I met some gypsies coming down the road
and I had to hide in a cornfield until they went past.
Ma'd said gypsies liked to steal little kids.
The next spring we moved to another farm across the road.
I wanted to stay home because Uncle Herm
had come all the way from Orange City to help us.
He was the best one to play with I ever had.
Pa said no. "Go to school, boy,
march, walk chalk, hurry now, get."
I bawled my head off. I was a bullhead.
I hid in the cob-shed until Ma found me.
Ma said, "You better not let your pa catch you home."
Finally I went up the road and over the hill.
When I came to our mailbox I stopped.
I wanted to play with my Uncle Herm.
I ate my lunch before the mailman came around.
The neighbor lady Mrs. Berg came and got her mail
and then went home and telephoned my ma
and told her I was playing hooky under the mailbox.
Pretty soon over the hill came Pa in a wagon.
He had a whip and was cussing blue blazes.
He got out of the wagon while Uncle Herm held the lines
and whipped me up the road past Berg's.
"I'll show you who's boss around here."
When I got to school I was still sighing big sighs.

The other kids were eating from their dinner buckets.
I went out to the privy and locked myself in for a while.

The next winter Aunt Kathryn moved in with us.
She taught in our school.
She was strict but she liked us.
She was easy on Ed but held me down.
One of the Reilly boys caught a field mouse
and put him in a Bull Durham tobacco sack.
He asked me if I dared to let it out
while Aunt Kathryn played the organ.
I said, "Sure, give him to me."
I let the mouse out just when Aunt Kathryn
was singing, "O say can you see."
The mouse ran straight for the organ.
Aunt Kathryn jumped on top of the organ seat
and screamed her head off.
Everbody pitched in to help catch the mouse.
I was the one who finally tailed him.
Afterwards, when it was quiet again,
the friendly Berg girl raised her hand
and told Aunt Kathryn who let the mouse out.
Ma gave me an awful tongue-hiding when I got home.
But Pa, he almost laughed his head off.
He told all the neighbors about it
and he and I became pretty good friends again.

We had a real dock-the-rock blizzard the next winter.
It made more noise than a thousand howling wolves.
Pa got stuck in it coming home from Doon,
so I pitched in and tackled the chores.
I even milked one of the cows, Three-Tit.
When Pa came home and found the chores done
except for milking the tough cows,
his eyes looked like two holes in the cookstove.
The next morning he woke me at five
and asked in a kind voice
if I'd like to have two legs of coffee with him.
Later he asked if all three of my hands were working.
"Because if they are, from now on you can milk Three-Tit."

One day I heard a commotion in the house.
I was playing making hay with Rover and my red wagon.
I went into the house to see what was wrong.

There was Ma wringing her hands and wondering what to do.
My brother Floyd was slowly turning purple.
He kept twisting around on the horsehair couch.
''Frederick, run and get your pa quick.
    Floyd's got the convulsions. Hurry quick.''
I stared at Floyd.
It looked about as awful as it sounded.
I ran through the grove and down the end of the field.
I ran until my breath came out like a blowtorch.
Pa saw me coming and stopped his horses.
''What's the matter, boy?
    Did they finally hang the Kaiser?''
''Floyd's got the convulsions!''
The way Pa's face fell it was like
seeing a pheasant shot on the rise.
''Hop up here, kid, and we'll hit for home galley west.''
The horses ran like a couple of whirlwinds.
The cultivator shovels clattered against the yellow wheels.
We hit the yard doing thirty per.
Four big steps and Pa was in the house.
Pa picked Floyd up, called his name.
Pa had a voice that went through you like a steam whistle.
He could have waked the dead with it.
All of a sudden Floyd began to cry,
and his black face went back to being red again.
''Better call the doctor, don't you think?'' Ma said.
''Why didn't you ring him in the first place?'' Pa said.
Ma started to cry. ''I was so worried. We got so many debts.''
Pa cussed. ''Anyway, Floyd is crying good now.''

We next moved to a place east of Doon.
Pa bought us a branded horse named Tip
and built a box on a buggy running gear
so we could ride warm to school.
One day at noon
in the middle of the winter
our hired man Gerrit showed up at school.
A terrible yellow blizzard was coming, he said,
and we better hustle home.
We piled in and made old Tip run as fast as she could go.
Gerrit rode his horse ahead of us.
About halfway home the yellow storm turned white.
Gerrit tied a hitching strap
from the horn of his saddle to Tip's bridle.
He bucked ahead of us into the northeast wind.

But when we got to the Little Rock bridge
we had to give up.
Gerrit took us down a side lane where his folks lived
and got us kids safe on the yard just in time.
I helped Gerrit put the horses in the barn.
We almost got lost crossing the yard on the way back.
The wind howled all night, worse than cooped up coyotes.
The next morning I had breakfast with Gerrit's folks.
They served fat with syrup.
You ate it by dipping your bread in it.
Trouble was, they served beef fat, not hog fat,
and they served it cold so that white rings
formed along the edges of the puddle of it.
It made me sick to my stomach.
That noon in school I vomited into the hot air register.
All in all, it turned out to be quite a winter storm.

The winter I turned eleven
I read through the new class books the first week,
then had nothing to do except arithmetic.
Our principal chewed the corner of his mouth awhile,
then made me take the sixth
and the seventh grades at the same time.
The school was full of cousins that year
and they asked their parents if that was fair.
Man alive!
At church they looked at me like I was a skink,
instead of what I was, a country love boy.
I had to play dumb sometimes,
hit singles instead of homers,
so I could keep my cousins for friends.
Lucky for me my heels hurt bad that summer
and my cousins won all the footraces.
That was the year I began to read books
under the quilts with a flashlight at night
so not even Pa would know about me reading.

I was barely twelve
when the relatives began to pester Pa
about me going to high school.
''More schoolin' will only turn him agin you, Frank.
    By the sweat of his brow,
    I say, make him work like my kids are gonna.
    By the sweat of his brow.
    You're not gonna let him go just when

he's about to begin earning his oats, are you?
Making up them rimes for the principal—
what'll he do when he gets through high school, write books?
For godsakes.''
Pa had always called me his special hired hand,
and he'd thought a lot about keeping me home,
but it was Ma who made up his mind
and shut up the relatives
and made me happy.
''The Lord will not hold us guiltless
     if we let the boy bury his talent in a cornfield.
     It would be nice if our son could become a domeny.
     Or maybe even a teacher in the Christian school.''
I didn't know about the minister part of it,
nor even about that teacher business,
but I did know I was hungry for something far away—
even to reading the Monkey Ward catalogue
out in the privy Sunday mornings.

Thirteen is an unlucky number for some people.
It wasn't for me.
I'd always had a special girl
ever since I could remember,
someone to meet eyes with in church on Sunday,
or brush against in town on Saturday.
When I turned thirteen I learned
I wanted to do more than just meet eyes with a girl.
I wanted to become dreamy with a girl. Alone.
Every time a family came over to visit us
and we kids played wink or hide-and-seek
I tried to get the best-looking girl
to snuggle alone in the weeds with me.
I mooned around with her some,
but it never did any good.
In high school the older girls giggled funny
when I passed love poems to them.
Yes, the dreamy part was good.
I smelled yeast and wild roses
all day long those days.

The fall I was a junior at the academy
two clouds had a collision east of Hull.
I was working my way through school on a dairy,
milking twenty-six cows in the morning,

the same hundred four tits at night,
delivering milk bottles on the run.
The cloudburst tried to cross the pasture
behind the barn all in one big push.
The next morning after milking
I worked all day long fixing a line fence,
standing hip-deep in cold sliding water,
my mouth full of cold staples,
cold nippers in one hand,
a slippery hammer in the other.
Man, it was good to be pinching
all those warm tits that night.
I finally even drank some of the warm milk,
right there in the barn out of the bucket.
I had never liked milk much
after having watched Ed get all that titty.

Our church always had a big picnic
on Decoration Day by the Big Rock River.
There would be a parade in town in the morning,
guns going off,
hup ah hup right,
old mothers crying,
halt one two three,
the flag shining high,
boom!
our honored dead!
and then we'd drive out to Brower's pasture.
We'd first play burn-out catch,
and knock up flies that would hang in the air
for all the world like chicken hawks,
then eat a couple of plates of potato salad,
beans and wieners and pie and icecream,
then play a real ball game.
By the time I was fifteen I'd developed
a pretty good sidearm curve.
So the single men asked me
if I would pitch against the married men.
We skunked the old stiffs for seven innings.
Then in the eighth they tied it up five to five.
When the married men loaded the bases in the ninth
Uncle Herm came running over from shortstop
looking like he'd had some poisoned pie.
"Don't you care?" he cried. "Don't you care to win?

Is that what that academy did to you?
　　Give you the big head instead of a good curve?''
Well, I got mad
and threw my curve straight overhand
and with my new drop struck out the side.
In the eleventh our catcher hit a triple
and scored on a wild pitch by Pa.
Afterwards even the minister came over
and shook my hand in both of his.
I really had the big head for a long time after that.

By the time I was sixteen
all of my brothers had arrived:
Edward, Floyd, John, Abben, Henry.
I got along with all of them pretty good.
We played ball with the calf-barn for a backstop.
We hayed and shocked and picked corn together.
We sat in descending order around the table.
We sat together in church on Sunday,
Pa and I on either end of the pew
and Ma in the middle with the kids.
We wrestled on the grass in the evening,
all five brothers trying to get me down,
even baby Henry in his wet pants,
and when they couldn't quite make it,
Pa would sometimes pitch in and help,
sitting on one of my shoulders.
Of them all only Floyd didn't like it too well
that I was boss when the folks were gone.
We got into a pushing argument one day
while watering the work horses by the tank.
Floyd said, ''Think you're so smart, graduating from high school.
You're not the only bull nuts around here, you know.
Get your dang plugs over
so I can water my horses too.''
Well, of course, I pushed back.
''Floyd, trouble with you is,
　　you're just a big dripnose balk-head.''
Well, that started it off. We both
dropped the hitching straps and went at it.
He surprised me with how strong he was.
When he really got mad he had man muscles.
We pushed and grunted back and forth,
through cow pies,

over a little strawpile,
finally into a puddle next to the tank.
It made me laugh to discover
he really was a tough bull too.
I was proud of him.
He was my brother.
Finally he got his arms around my middle
and I let him sling me around a little
so that it happened I stumbled
and we fell backwards into the water tank.
We came up out of the cold water
blowing green moss out of our noses.
We were both laughing our heads off.
Pa had watched it all from the porch stoop.
He got up and ambled over.
"So! not so strong as you thought you was, ha, Fred?
   Good work, Floyd. That'll teach him."
After that Floyd and I were real good friends.

Seventeen, and a loud call up the stairwell.
"Hurry, Frank! hurry, Fred!
   or you'll never see Alice alive on earth again!"
It was Uncle Hank calling.
He had offered to sit by Ma until dawn.
Pa and I bumped into each other in the dark
as we turned into the bedroom together,
pulling on our clothes as we ran.
We were too late.
Too late.
The heart had already stopped beating.
The cheeks were already losing their color,
slowly turning into unlined parchment.
Slowly the brow smoothed over,
the lips began to smile ever so little,
the features slowly changed
into an expression of settled majesty.
It was done. Gone. Dead.
Little Henry, two years old,
played in his crib within arm's reach of her.
He shook his rattle,
showed his dead mother
how his teddybear could stand by hisself,
asked if he could have a cookie,
pretty soon said he had to go to the toidy.

The sun was up when I laced up my bluchers
on the cellar door outside under the bay window.
I called up the cows and the horses.
After I'd stanchioned and haltered them,
I sat down on a milk stool
and began to miss her.

I pitched alfalfa all day long,
I drove all the way to Hills,
pitched a heartbreaker of a game,
then drove all the way back in my percolator Ford.
When I stepped across the yard in the dark
I found my pa sitting on the cellar step
with the housekeeper, hand in hand.
Seeing them together it broke my step.
Pa said, ''Well, Fred, guess I might as well tell you.
Hattie and I got married today.''
I heard a great branch break off a tree—
yet there wasn't as much as a baby's breath of wind out.
My tongue had nothing to say.
In the dark my eyes didn't either.
Pa said, ''Ain't you gonna congratulate us?''
Finally my tongue did talk.
''Congratulations.''
My new ma said,
''Ya, Pa and I thought it best we got married
    before people began to talk.''
Before people began to talk?
I heard the great branch
hit the ground with a splashing sound.
I went upstairs to our room.
I sat on the edge of my bed.
I heard all my sleeping brothers
breathing steadily and serenely around me.
I pulled at my nose with my thumb and forefinger.
Crickets were singing outdoors.
A new ma.
I was free.
Cut off.
Free to go to college.
Provided I worked my way through.
But free.
Eighteen winters and free.

"Eighteen winters and free."

FREDERICK MANFRED, 18, 1930.

Richard Bissell

"WHEN I was a boy, there was but one permanent ambition among my comrades in our village on the west bank of the Mississippi River. That was to be a steamboatman," said Mark Twain in *Life on the Mississippi*. "I went on the river because I liked boats all my life and I liked the river," said Richard Bissell in *My Life on the Mississippi, or Why I Am Not Mark Twain* (1973). "I liked the smell of engine rooms and I liked river people and I liked the talk."

Richard Bissell could scarcely have avoided liking the Mississippi. Like the older American writer to whom he has been compared and to whom he has compared himself, he grew up along the Mississippi at Dubuque, where he was born in 1913. Five of his dozen books, including his first one, *A Stretch on the River* (1950) are about rivers—the Mississippi, the Ohio, the Monongahela.

For all that, Bissell's fame came from a novel, *7½ Cents* (1953) and its stage and film musical versions, *Pajama Game,* which are based on the family garment business established by Bissell's great-grandfather in Dubuque in 1845. *7½ Cents* is not as good a book as *A Stretch on the River,* but it led to his moving to New York and Connecticut and a second musical, *Say, Darling* (1958). Still, his love affair with the river continued and he spent his summers there, piloting his tugboat up and down the river. Bissell died in Dubuque, near his river, in the spring of 1977.

It seems appropriate then to offer, in place of the essay I hoped Bissell would write, "Not a Difficult Feat, Even for a Boy," from *My Life on the Mississippi,* a piece that reflects a result of his early affection for the river.

NOT A DIFFICULT FEAT,
EVEN FOR A BOY

THE FIRST boat I built was in our cellar out there on the farm three miles from the Mississippi at the top of the hill above Catfish Creek. Built it nights with my buddy Earl when we were fourteen years old. The teachers called him Earl and the girls who were sweet on him and the rest of us called him Oke because he came up from Oklahoma when he was eight years old. It is tough to have a buddy that can beat you at everything but he could. I was a runt. . . .

His mother had a .45 caliber Oklahoma state trooper's revolver and she could put two holes in a soup can if you threw it in the air. Or one anyway. Actually I don't think she even had a revolver but brother Mycroft started the soup-can legend somehow and then of course we couldn't let it go.

Earl had a young brother we called "the Beaver" because he had a big nose though I don't know what that has to do with beavers. He subsequently went back to Oklahoma and got to be a state trooper.

As for love we were both in love with somebody from eight years on and that included two of the teachers, Clara Bow, and above all Phyllis Haver. Actually I am still in love with Phyllis Haver.

We built that rowboat in the cellar talking about Phyllis Haver and allied subjects dating back to Egyptian times. Earl would kid me about going to dancing class. I liked dancing class just fine but of course I had to pretend to him that I didn't.

"Don't kid me," he would say. "You know you like it, dancing with Billie Jane and her bumps."

"You better look out if you don't wanna good punch in the snoot."

"Who's gonna do it? You awready told me bout dancing with Billie Jane, and her bumps, too."

"Aw dry up."

Then my father would come down to throw a few scoops of coal into the furnace and raise hell with the poker and the grates and he would say: "Don't butt those bottom boards up so tight they will swell up and buckle. How is your father, Earl, is he home this week?"

"No, sir, he is on the Road, he is out on the Minnesota territory this week," Oke would say.

"Well he is pushing a very fine line of goods," Father would say and go upstairs and continue reading "Do You Sell Them or Do They Have to Buy?" ("Napoleon was a salesman, Christ was . . .")

Oke even called his own father "sir." I guess that was Southern. His father came from Louisiana and smoked Picayune cigarettes. He moved in an entirely different circle than my father and played poker up on Kimball's Island across from Eagle Point at Doc Pettigrew's cottage, and drank bootleg gin and ginger ale, and knew all sorts of strange people—bootleggers, commercial fishermen, circus people, railroad engineers, sleazy doctors, oil-stock promoters, baseball players . . . and he was not home much of the time.

My father did not drink and resented the rituals of Prohibition-time drinking when Pete Karberg would invite the men out to the pantry before some dinner party and with winks and nudges and remarks about "the real stuff," "right from Canada," etc., he would pour out "a little nip" all around. I suppose Father would take "a little snort to keep the cold out" under those circumstances, but he never kept booze at home and never invited the boys out to the pantry.

After Prohibition Father mellowed a good deal and got whiskey from the Iowa State liquor control for himself and the boys and 89 cent sherry for Mother who never accepted a glass without saying "I'm sure this will make me tipsy."

One time when I was twenty-six years old and Mycroft was twenty-nine, Mother and Father and Mycroft and my wife and I stopped in Guttenberg, Iowa, a very nice old rivertown north of Dubuque, on our way down from Lake Superior. "All right boys, let's have a beer," Father said and we went into a saloon and had a 10 cent beer apiece. When we got back to the car Mother said, "Now Fred, you will have to drive, the boys have been drinking."

Guttenberg has some handsome stone houses and a front street right on the river. Dubuque hasn't got that, the river front is all industrial. Guttenberg is also the present home of the former highly precocious Elsie Katzenbach who wrote me an extremely incendiary note in junior high school which my mother found in my pocket. Also the home of Elvira Hedstrom who I was on a double date with one night when Cap Molo managed to run into the East Dubuque bridge abutment. When the cops came he gave his famous imitation of the steamer *Harriet* making a landing in a high wind. But the cops all knew who was who back then and they just told us to go home and not run into the bridge anymore if we could help it.

East Dubuque was a ripsnorter in those days and had slots, craps, and

"Now, the way to get a boat is to make it."

BISSELL, AGE 16, IN THE BOAT.

three or four roulette wheels. It was wide open and three miles from town even had Bonbon McClure's place, a first class whorehouse with girls from Chicago. Bonbon got killed in a fight in East Moline, Illinois. There is still a strip in East Dubuque, with deafening music pits and girls up there wiggling but the gambling is all over. A new governor of Illinois came in on a "Spoil the Fun" ticket, and whether he is still in or not I don't know but the wheels and the merry bouncing of the dice never came back.

And the Hilltop Casino—a tawdry night club of happy memory where the lights burned long, the steaks were tough, the drummer played loud and the MC and the entertainers sweated blood—is gone. When I was home on vacation from steamboating we always headed for East Dubuque and for the Hilltop. The Hilltop was a roadhouse in the best true sense. I often have a crying spell when I think of the nights I have spent half-crocked at Hilltop, looking down the table at my dear friends Tom, Betty, Eddie, Mary, Mycroft, Susie, Courty, Velma, Woody, Jean, Scoop, Heebers, Sis, Marge, John, Angela, Bill, Lenore, Dunc, Pat—that's enough—and across to the minuscule stage where a girl with tassels on her tits is playing a musical staircase with her feet while tossing Indian clubs. Russ Evans is on the drums and giving her all the rim shots she needs. A girl at the next table rotates her head slowly as though it was on a turntable and winks at me. Outside people are "necking" in cars, or possibly "petting." Yes, actually "petting." Gives you goose bumps don't it?

You don't get no goose bumps out of *Oh Calcutta,* just a slight lingering headache.

Twenty-six years after I built my boat, I was a writer and I wrote the book for a Broadway show produced by Boy-Wonder Boy-Millionaire Boy-Producer Hal Prince. He and I were big old good buddies—he is a very funny guy especially for a producer, and we invited him out to Dubuque one summer when we were there. After I moved away I still kept a houseboat there and I still do, a big steel houseboat 80 feet long.

Hal Prince is a lovely human being but Dubuque is pretty far from Sardi's and I don't think he had a very good time. Dubuque can be very strong medicine for an outsider especially from New York City. And in summer it gets HOT. Mark Twain went to Keokuk, Iowa, in the summer of 1886 to see his aged mother, Jane Clemens. All Sam Clemens had to say about the visit was that it was hot. Keokuk is downriver a ways from Dubuque.

"Keokuk weather was pretty hot. Jean and Clara sat up in bed and cried about it, and so did I. Well it did need cooling; I remember I burnt a hole in my shirt, there, with some ice cream that fell on it."

Hilltop Casino was one of the principal places in Dubuque that Hal Prince didn't really understand. It didn't fit the script, the casting was bad, and all the actors were overboard. But you can't much blame him—it was 95 and 100 degrees all the time he was there in Dubuque and people kept telling him things like "The Langworthy house is the first octagon house west of the Mississippi," and "You wait and see, Iowa is going to beat Minnesota by two touchdowns this year," and brother Mycroft said, "Now you take pompano for example, actually it's not a damn bit better than catfish." So we went to East Dubuque to Eddie Lyons for catfish and, while Hal plucked hopefully at the fish, Eddie sang "Little Sir Echo" in his burlesque-house tenor.

"Listen Hal," Mycroft said, "he knows the guy who wrote that song."

"Who wrote it?" says Hal.

"I don't know," says Mycroft. "Some guy. He knows him. He knows a lot of people in show business. You oughtta talk to him. I'll introduce you.''

Then we took Hal to the Dubuque Golf and Country Club and Mycroft introduced him to the bartender. This is one of the highest honors that can come to any visitor to Dubuque. What with the heat and the catfish and "Little Sir Echo" Hal was in kind of a daze by now, and when Eddie Frudden came up and said he knew him from someplace was he in the Navy in 1944, Hal somehow ordered, or got, a sidecar by mistake. So Mycroft started ordering sidecars.

You can't enjoy Dubuque on sidecars, as I have tried it many times and all it got me was a threat of divorce proceedings.

The way you built a boat when I was a kid was to get a book. Nobody was going to show you how, as togetherness in re boat building had not been invented yet. Plenty of togetherness about washing the car and weeding the bean patch but not building a skiff.

My book was *The American Boy's Handy Book* by Dan Beard. In the flyleaf, in a spidery female hand were written the words:

> *Frederick*
> *from*
> *Papa and Mama*
> *January 24, 1890*

My father's twelfth birthday.

This book had been around a long time but it had held up remarkably well considering Father as a boy had got glue on it when making the Giant Chinese Warrior Kite, sawdust in it when he made the Tom Thumb Ice Boat, and paint on page 361 when he constructed the Rainbow Whirlygig. Mycroft and I had also often pummeled it around and left it in the garage and in our tree house but mostly we just looked at it because the projects seemed impossible.

"Procure three twelve inch clear pine boards eighteen feet long . . ."

Now where would we get three pine boards eighteen feet long?

"Next get the blacksmith to make you four iron straps . . ."

WHAT blacksmith? And who was to pay him?

"The grocer will be glad to give you a Chinese tea chest . . ."

Mr. Helbing had a lot of penny candy and Rath's ham sausage but hadn't seen a tea chest since the Spanish American War.

What kind of American Boys were these who could summon up eighteen foot clear pine boards, blacksmiths and tea chests? They were the same kind of boys no doubt who were constantly finding wealthy old gentlemen's pocketbooks in the pages of Horatio Alger, Jr. Horatio Alger was not available at the Carnegie-Stout Public Library under the bluff on

11th Street, but could be procured at the Kresge store at Eighth and Main streets for 10 cents a volume.

But these Horatio Alger heroes all had widowed mothers and a young sister named Nelly to support. If Father had had my interests at heart he would have produced for me a sister named Nelly and left Mother a widow without funds, and by now I would be president of the American Brake Shoe Co.

So neither Mycroft nor I ever dreamed of *making* anything from this book. It was just reading matter, especially the three-story squirrel house with cupola that would ''give room for a whole family of squirrels,'' and the ''Boys' Own Houseboat,'' proprietorship of which was as remote from me as that of the Wurlitzer saxophone with pearl keys which sneered at me from the pages of *Boys' Life* every month.

One day after gulping a bit, while Father was reading the *Telegraph-Herald-and-Times-Journal* and smoking a Melachrino, I asked him if I could buy a boat. He had just read the daily Abe Martin gem out loud and said ''Pretty good.''

''Listen Dad,'' I said, after laughing heartily at Abe Martin which I did not understand why it was funny in the slightest, ''can I buy a boat Al Kempf knows a guy who will sell his rowboat for eleven dollars with oars and everything and I have eight dollars in the school savings bank and I can earn some more and this is a real keen boat Al saw it at the Peosta boat club and it is painted red and white and has oars and everything how about it Dad can I buy it huh if I get it I won't even go out on the river I will keep it down on Catfish Creek below Swallow Bank and Newton's place gee Dad how about it every kid ought to have a boat it says in *Boys' Life* that owning a boat builds character and just think, if Mark Twain had never had a boat when he was a boy he probly never would have written *Tom Sawyer* and *Life on the Mississippi* can I buy it what about it Dad?''

''How long have you been rehearsing that?'' he said.

''Now Fred don't be a tease,'' Mother said, putting down the *Delineator*.

''Sam Clemens never had a skiff when he was a boy down in Hannibal, they were bone poor. His father was a typical example of a helpless intellectual trapped on the American frontier.''

''My father always said he was no gentleman,'' Mother said.

''Where is my old copy of Dan Beard?'' Father said. ''Go and get it. Edith, your father as a literary critic leaves something to be desired. Walt Whitman was not a gentleman, Dostoevsky was not a gentleman, Voltaire was not a gentleman, Balzac was not a gentleman, and by your father's standards William Shakespeare was not a gentleman—that is to say he did not eat at Henrici's, play poker at the Chicago Athletic Club, or write letters to the Chicago *Tribune*.''

By the time I got back with the book Mother was saying, ''I don't think that's a very nice way to talk about my father in front of the boy.''

"Your father is all right. I like him," Father said. "Forget about it. Give me the book.

"Now," he said, "the way to get a boat is to make it. Here we are, look at this. 'The Scow. To build a scow-shaped row boat is not a difficult feat, even for a boy. And when it is finished he will find it a very convenient boat, roomy, and not hard to row.' That's the ticket, that's what you want."

"Gee Dad," I said, "I don't know how to make a boat. Will you help me?"

"Not on your life," he said. "But I will foot the lumber bill."

"Crimanentlys," I replied.

And that's how I got my first boat. But we didn't build a scow we built what Dan Beard called a "Yankee Pine," with a pointed bow and some sheer to it. I still have the lumber bill—I throw away *nothing*.

I always kept notebooks, log books, diaries and lists of things I wanted and things I wanted to do sometime. I still have them.

In one of my notebooks for the year 1928 after we built the boat I find the following:

Saturday April 21—
Embarked at 9:30 AM from Dubuque ice harbor for Dubuque's Grave. Passed steamers *J. W. Weeks* and *C. C. Webber.* Captain Bissell rowing alone. Picked up Al and arrived Catfish Creek 11:30 AM. Beached at Newton's farmhouse picked up Oke rowed up to Rockdale. Tied up. Went to general store for eats and pop. Back to farmhouse. Put stuff in shed and left. Walked home. Al's dog, Sport, with us and Oke's puppy named Buster.

We walked four miles home and were very happy. In this same log book of mine there is a very definite parallel with Mark Twain's desire for command and the right to issue "crisp orders." It says "The captain will have complete authority over his men while in boat *and on way home from boating.*"

I am sorry there are no funny boyish misspellings. I know it is against all the rules of boyhood writing but it can't be helped. I was an un-American Boy and a disappointment to everyone because I refused to go along with the Real Boy tradition. I spelled things right and I never played marbles. But don't worry, I chawed tobacker and put rocks in snowballs and did all those other comical things that Real Boys are supposed to do.

That was a nice little boat and it cost 13 dollars for lumber, white lead, cotton, paint, oarlocks and oars. When he was fourteen years old my son Nat said he would shrivel up and die right away if he didn't have a water-ski boat like the other guys. I hate shriveled young people so I quick bought him a boat and it cost me 900 dollars.

Or — —
as Andre Gide said on his deathbed: "Before you quote me, make sure I'm conscious."

🌸 🌸 Paul Corey

IN THE LAST couple of years, moose have been sighted on two different occasions in Iowa, and here and there the tourist will see an occasional small herd of buffalo in some farmer's field or encounter a deer in the glare of headlights. These are reminders outside of zoos that once upon a time what came to be domesticated Iowa was part of the wilderness—a vast area of plains, lakes, ponds, and rivers—inhabited only by the Indian and wild animals.

The white settlers came upon the land in the 1830s after the Black Hawk treaty. By 1890, as Allan G. Bogue has told us, the prairie had become farmland. The Indian's domain was restricted, the buffalo had all but disappeared, the passenger pigeon was extinct, and other small animals were fighting for survival.

Among these were the wolf and the coyote. With their natural food supplies diminishing, these critters turned to farmers' herds and flocks—sheep, pigs, calves, colts, chickens, turkeys, ducks, and geese. To the farmer trying to survive in a struggle with an often hostile natural environment, wolves and coyotes represented a portion of that hostile world that could be dealt with.

Moreover, a folklore, at least some of it brought to the new world from the old, grew around the wolf. Tales were told of heroic individuals surviving attacks by wolf packs by building small fires or lighting one match after another through a dark night and taller tales of wolf packs pursuing sleighs, nipping at the horses' legs, trying to hamstring them. Bolder animals tried to leap aboard the sleighs as they caromed over the frosty snow. In the most incredible of these tales, desperate pioneers tossed out parcels of food bought at the remote market town, or even more incredibly, threw babies to the blood-crazed packs. Many of these tales made their way into the printed literature of the prairies—into newspapers, books, and magazines. I heard them in far-off Montana, one night in December 1918, after we had been trailed by a solitary scrawny wolf as we sleighed up a canyon looking for our Christmas tree. There they were told as true incidents that had happened to farmers and ranchers in the area.

A half century or longer ago, farmers combined their efforts to rid their lands of the wily animals by organizing wolf and coyote hunts. A cordon of armed men, boys, and an occasional female was positioned around a mile square of land. Beginning at the edges of the roads, these hunters worked toward the center, their dogs sniffing, yapping, and racing here and there as they came upon a scent.

Two Iowa writers have used the wolf hunt as chapters in novels about farming in Iowa. Frederick Manfred's gory tale can be found in *This Is the Year* (1947). Paul Corey's tale follows. When I first asked Paul to contribute a piece for this collection, he said he thought that Curt Harnack's *We Have All Gone Away* (1973) had said it all. But I reminded Corey that there was nothing in Harnack's book that came close to the wolf hunt. So he agreed to the use of "The Hunt" from his book, *The Road Returns* (1940), noting that the language used is common to 1922.

Paul Corey, author of fourteen books and many shorter stories and book reviews, was born in Shelby County, Iowa, the scene of the hunt described here as well as the scene of

THE HUNT

four books about farm life in Iowa a half century ago or longer. He grew up on a 160-acre farm near Atlantic and worked his way through the University of Iowa. Since graduation in 1925, he has lived either in the East or (since 1947) in Sonoma, California, not far from the Jack London ranch in the Valley of the Moon.

Roy Meyer, in *The Middle-Western Farm Novel in the Twentieth Century* (1965), says that Corey's farm novels are "among the most important contributions made during the past generation to farm fiction."

THE FIRST Wednesday in December, both Mena and Ira came bouncing over to Otto's desk in the study hall before nine o'clock.

"Can you come out Friday, Ot?" cried Mena. "There's going to be a wolf hunt."

"Wolf hunt?" Otto looked skeptical. "And elephants?"

"No kiddin'," said Ira. "Coyotes have been killin' sheep—Lang's, John Haas's—Cec Tyler's organizin' a hunt. Two-three hundred of us're goin' to line up across the valley and work down the railroad tracks."

"Can you come, Ot?" urged Mena.

"You goin' to hunt?" Otto asked her.

"Sure."

Ira frowned. "Don't think you'd better, sis."

"Well, I am. You'll come, won't you, Ot?"

Otto rode out with them Friday evening, taking with him the family's twelve-gauge shotgun. He breathed the cold air deeply as if to chill himself and make the coziness of the Crosby house more enjoyable. He liked the large comfortableness of Mrs. Crosby, and to make conversation with Ed, he asked how things were on the farm.

"Tough sleddin' now, Ot," said Crosby, and his fingers worried the mole on his cheek.

Otto noticed how withered and battered Ed was; he knew that the Crosbys were having a hard time making ends meet. They no longer kept a hired girl and Jens Jepsen had left them a year ago and hadn't been

". . . a thin layer of snow
lay over the hills and
valleys, crunchy and frost
crisp . . ."

replaced. The only help Ed had besides Harry and Ira was Sam Barret, the married man he kept on the old Frazier place.

After supper when Mena started to get her knickers ready, Harry raised a protest: "Listen, Mena, you ain't goin'."

"Why not?"

"She can handle a gun," put in Otto.

Harry snorted. "You've just got a crush on her, that's all." He turned to his father: "Dad, tell Mena she can't go."

State Historical Society of Iowa collection

"Mena can take care of herself," replied Ed.

"Well," grumbled Harry, "you'll have to look out for her, Ot. She's your responsibility."

"I'll keep her under my wing," Otto said.

"I don't need anybody's wing," snapped the girl and jerked her shoulder scornfully at him.

They were up long before dawn and had the chores done; a thin layer of snow lay over the hills and valleys, crunchy and frost crisp, and overhead the stars shone with a cold green brightness. Around the breakfast table the family and Otto ate pancakes, sausage, and drank coffee with appetite, the breakfast fragrance filling the hot room. Would the car start, would they really kick up a coyote? They'd probably shoot plenty of rabbits, anyhow.

It was still dark when they arrived at the country store; the road intersection was already crowded with men and boys. Wives were there with the family cars ready to take their menfolks to the starting point for the hunt. Headlights flashed on cold, red, excited faces, gleamed on gun barrels and revealed caps pulled low over ears, collars turned up. Dogs ran around sniffing strange dogs, yapping, snarling, fighting. Eyes continually searched the east for dawn, while white-mittened hands flapped together to loosen frost-stiffened fingers.

Mena stayed close to Otto. Now that she was here in this crowd, her bravado had vanished and her elbow was never far from his. He squared his shoulders being masculine and protective; his eyes searched the throng for faces he knew: Mel Wallace, Dale Lang, Roy Tyler, Bud Wheeler, Harry Clausen, and he nodded when they recognized him. He seemed to be trying to find the pulse of this crowd—to feel a oneness with them. He heard scraps of talk about the bank failure in Elm, about hard times; he saw someone tipping a bottle to his lips and knew this was local hooch made by farmers to help pay their debts. But over all this he felt the excitement, the charged atmosphere of a mass of human beings assembled, determined on a plan of action, determined to accomplish something. And Otto felt a kindling warmth inside him, and he smiled down at Mena proud of her being beside him.

More cars arrived. The horizon to the east paled, throwing into relief the bare-branched trees above the milling throng. Someone said: "Let's get goin', we'll freeze to death standin' here." A group started a bonfire with old boxes from behind the country store. Cigarettes and pipes glowed in the morning dusk like strange winter fireflies. Shouts and laughter rose as the intersection grew jammed tighter with the hunters.

Then Cecil Tyler climbed to the porch of the meeting hall and bellowed for attention. He called out the names of thirty farmers—they were the captains—each was to take ten fellows and spread out on a line a mile and a half each side of the Little Bad River. Occasionally the dawn light gleamed on the hook protruding from his left sleeve and showed the red faces of the crowd tilted upward listening to him.

The three Crosbys and Otto joined Mel Wallace's squad which included old man Farrel, Neils Neffsen, Clarence Baumgarten and two of the Dugan boys. Mel looked them over. "Hello, Ot," he said; "how's your mother?" Then he recognized Mena: "You huntin' with us, Mena?"

"Sure," Otto said. "Why not?"

The others looked doubtful; Mel frowned, then said: "Well, guess Ed's girl can throw shot as well as anybody else."

Tyler ordered everybody to their positions and Ed Crosby loaded all of Wallace's squad into the car and took them to their position about a mile west of the river. They climbed the fence to the south and Wallace ordered them to spread out in a line about fifty feet apart. Ira Crosby was far to the right, then Mena, then Otto, then Harry next to Wallace. Their starting point was on a high ridge; it was almost daylight now and they could see far over the surrounding land, and down the valley to the railroad tracks eight miles away. A freight train chuffed up the grade west; they saw a steam-white plume, then heard the long-drawn blast of the whistle which echoed against the rolling snow-covered hills as if they were metal.

Some of them started to move out but Wallace told them they had to wait for the signal. Otto could see Mena's face now, her cheeks as red as apples. "Ain't we got fun?" he called to her and she grinned, brushing back her bobbed hair beneath a red tam. The butt of her gun rested on the toe of her high lace boot and she slouched boyishly. She's just like another fellow being along, he thought, and was amazed to discover that a girl could be like that.

From the last group over came a yell: "Let's go!"

The shout was relayed along the line, echoing far through the clear air. Wallace climbed a fencepost and looked toward the river. "Hold it!" he yelled. He stood up straight on the post, his blue denim overalls and jacket bright in the dawn, his helmet pulled tight under his chin. His breath clouded up white in the still air. He became conscious of his conspicuousness and suddenly flapped his arms and crowed. Old man Farrel yelled, "Look out, you'll be taken for a crow." Laughter rang out; then the grumbling started again. What were they waiting for? it was light enough, wasn't it?

A distant boom echoed up from the river. "Let's go," shouted Wallace and jumped off his fencepost. "Keep in line now. Don't get ahead or behind—careful with your shootin'."

The long line of hunters started slowly, guns at the ready like skirmishing troops going into action. In movement, the chill morning air struck them harder, stinging their cheeks to an even brighter red. Down the front a gun boomed: someone had shot a rabbit. The line rose and fell like the crest of an irregular wave as it moved up over ridges and into hollows. From a high point, Otto could see the advancing hunters extending down across the river valley and up the far side, their distant progress emphasized by puffs of gun smoke and the belated report of the shot.

"The guys in the valley got the best hunting," groused Harry. Just then Ira's gun roared and he ran forward to pick up a kicking cottontail. A jackrabbit loped awkwardly up the ridge to the south, sat up a moment, the brown tips of his ears conspicuous, his white body blending with the snow. Harry took a long shot and he disappeared from sight.

The booming of guns came oftener now, focusing in spots—a cornfield or patch of weeds where the rabbits had burrowed. Sometimes the line lagged at a point while a patch was cleaned out. Dogs big and little ranged far in advance of the hunters, stirring up the game. Once a great white owl rose just ahead of Mena and soared over them snapping its beak.

Down a hollow to his left, Otto could see the Harris place, ahead was the Deidrick yard and to the right were the Crosby buildings perched on the ridge end above the Squaw Creek Valley. A cottontail bounced from beneath his feet, shooting like a bullet through the bent and stock-trampled cornstalks.

"Let him have it," yelled Harry.

Otto waited, then fired and the rabbit stopped and seemed to settle back in the snow.

"Good," Mena called.

They continued forward and when Otto came up with the animal, he picked it up and knocked off its head with one blow of the back of his hand. He carried it, the blood making a zig-zagging trail after him.

Someone yelled: "Where's the wolf?"

The line crossed the road running past the Crosbys' and School Number Nine. The sun was up now. The sound of gunfire quickened, then lagged, then quickened again. The man beyond Wallace yelled, "There he goes!" pointing to the Jensen pasture, but it was only a gray dog, hot on some trail.

"How you making out?" Otto called to Mena.

"Fine." She let her serious, intent face break into a grin.

Ahead now was the Squaw Creek Valley and down it to the left Otto could see the windbreak of the old home place. He would be crossing the northwest forty of the farm. He felt cold as memories came back to him: the lay of pasture land and cornfields, the barns and the corncrib he'd been so proud of. He remembered all the places where he used to hunt, the gullies where he had played Indian and cowboy and soldier. A rabbit jumped up to the right of him but he didn't notice until Harry's gunshot startled him.

The sector of his advance was taking him far to the west of the old farmyard, but his eyes scanned the place where it was behind its windbreak and the ridge. He could see the windmill in the valley below it. With a wave of his arm, he said to Mena: "There's the old home place."

"It's still there," she replied. She saw the half-woeful look on his face and added: "You miss it, Ot?"

"Sometimes." They were getting close together and Harry yelled: "Hey, none of this arm-in-arm stuff. I can't cover all the ground in between."

They pushed apart again. Otto wished that his group had passed closer to the farmyard. He hadn't set foot on it since they moved to town and a longing came over him to feel the shape of the ground there, a shape

*"He felt cold as memories came back to him:
the lay of pasture land and cornfields,
the barns and the corncrib he'd been so proud of."*

FARMYARD OF PAUL COREY'S BIRTHPLACE AT THE TIME OF THE HUNT.

that his feet would know again even in darkness. To make up for missing the yard, he searched for familiar spots in the section of the farm he was crossing: the gray broken horseweeds along the creek, the old bridge, the upward climb on the far side.

Harry kicked out a rabbit, fired at it and missed. Otto, still half-dreaming about the farm, fired and also missed. The cottontail raced through the broken cornstalks. Mena fired and it somersaulted to a stop ahead of Ira.

The boy yelled: "Who said Mena couldn't hunt?"

The line climbed the ridge, crossed the next road: this road goes past the home place and Wheelers', Otto told himself. Mena and he were skirting the Schief farmyard, but once on the far side they separated into position again. Guns had been roaring continuously all along the line; then from the direction of the river, following a lull, a shout echoed and a message was relayed along: "They've upped a coyote east of Murphys'."

Otto felt the coldness going out of him. From the top of the next ridge his glance swung eastward but he could see only the faint line of the hunters indicated by the blobs of smoke from their guns. Ahead was the

Thorne farmyard, and now they were moving into a long gully that angled upland to the southwest. Otto crossed the ditch and started up the next ridge; Harry was already across but Mena and Ira hadn't come to it yet. From the end of the gully on the meadow slope glided a small gray prairie wolf, cutting across the field toward the river. At first Otto thought it was a dog on a trail, head down, ears back; then he noticed its long brush tail. "Coyote!" he yelled. "Ira—Mena!"

Ira saw and blazed away, a long shot; Mena's gun roared. The coyote neared the top of the ridge above Otto and he let go both barrels; the kick on his shoulder was terrific. Harry added his fire. The coyote lurched as if he'd slipped in the snow, then disappeared over the ridge. Behind them in the gully, a dozen dogs yapped past, black, white, yellow and spotted bodies flowing like the wind, tongues lolling out, their cries rising and falling, growing louder as the scent grew hotter. The Crosbys and Otto were racing to the top of the ridge.

"We plugged him," Harry yelled.

"Darn near broke my shoulder," Otto panted.

Mena's eyes were like steel in their gleam and intensity. The dogs broke from the gully end and raced past them into the next arroyo where the coyote had disappeared. Wallace was yelling to the hunters on his left: "He's headin' that way!" But as the dogs plunged like a flood into the gully, the baying became yelps and roars, growls and snarls. When the hunters reached the ditch, the whole pack was attacking the wounded coyote. He snapped and tore viciously, sending mongrels yelping, licking their wounds. But it was a hopeless fight. The dogs closed in, tearing at him, smothering him, all trying to shake him. The steel snap of the wolf's jaws grew feeble as strength ebbed from his muscles; his gray coat gleamed with blood and the slavering from the jaws of the hunt-mad dogs. The fury of the pack did not lessen as they continued to maul the limp animal.

The line of hunters had broken and they crowded around the kill, excited voices jerking: "Got one! Boy-oh-boy! One less!" Mel Wallace tried to extricate the animal from the pack but the dogs weren't through with it. Some of them withdrew a little, sniffing one another, hackles standing; they seemed to be discussing the run, boasting to one another. Now and again a dog would rush at the limp wolf with a furious growl and shake it violently as if to show what he had done, to re-enact for the others the part he'd played or prove to them that he'd done it all by himself.

Wallace finally got the coyote away and put it in his bag. Then the excited mongrels ran circles sniffing the ground, sniffing and snapping at one another, barking—occasionally letting out a howl. They leaped at the bag on Mel's back until he kicked them off, shouting: "Get out of here, you–" He remembered that Mena Crosby was present. The dogs slunk away, circling again, looking for new scents. They were dogs strange to one another; they had only combined for this chase, it was each one for himself now. The hunters returned to their positions and continued the advance, shouting the news both ways along the line.

The sun was high now and Otto flung open his coat. They crossed the next east-west road and bore to the west to keep their distance from the river. Otto called to Mena: "Gettin' tired?"

"No," she answered.

The guns continued to roar, a cottontail dropped here, a jackrabbit there. In another creek valley someone shot a red squirrel. From the left came yells and over the ridge wafted the smell of a civet cat. Faces broke into grins and laughter echoed along the line.

Word came from the river valley that another coyote had been sighted. From the next ridge Otto surveyed the bottom to the southward. The railroad tracks were close now, less than four miles distant. He saw the eleven o'clock flyer sweeping down the grade from the west, the smoke lying low over the tops of the cars reminding him of the coyote's tail as it raced along the ridge.

Harry yelled: "There it goes!"

Across the distant pasture raced a pack of dogs and far ahead a single speck moved like the wind, heading west toward the hills. They saw it disappear into a shallow ditch. The baying of the pack had attracted other dogs roaming singly or in pairs all along the line and the animals began loping toward the river.

The hunters on the ridge paused to watch the scene in the bottom pasture. They saw the coyote doubling back, a gray fleeing speck on the bottom land, racing toward the river. On the upland, a yellow mongrel, with better than average eyesight, spotted the moving speck, let out a shrill yammering and plunged toward the valley after it. Other dogs followed him and soon a new pack was after the coyote. The line of hunters cut off the animal's escape upstream and the watchers on the ridge saw it dart into the brush along the river and a moment later emerge on the opposite side. It was headed for the eastern hills, but again it ran into dogs; a pack howling in from that side was soon on its heels and it doubled back toward the river once more. The hunters in the valley were moving toward the tornado of dogs at a run now.

The watchers on the ridge saw the coyote again break from the river brush and angle toward the hills to the northwest, but its swift flight was checked as the pack of dogs which had started on its trail came in from the west, cutting it off. The wolf bore to the right now, directly toward the running hunters; then it saw its danger and doubled again, but now the pack from the west saw it and their yelps became a joyous yammering. The second pack spotted it and the third pack, racing in from the east, made no attempt to follow the scent, but whirled in toward the other dogs. They were closing in now on a fanwise front and the coyote attempted to escape again to the west.

On the ridge the watchers hardly breathed, mouths hung open and eyes, hard as marbles, stared fascinated.

"Looket that wolf go," someone muttered, hardly knowing that he'd spoken.

A voice yelled: "He'll get away—he'll make it!"

"No—no, sir! Them three dogs comin' up on the right—boy are they travelin'!"

"They're closin'—he won't make it."

A shivering gasp went up from the watchers as below them they saw a whirlwind of dogs, like twisting autumn leaves, mill over the coyote.

"Oh, the poor thing," cried Mena and her mittened hand covered her mouth. Otto saw the sudden horror in her eyes.

"Guess that coyote'll kill no more sheep," said Harry.

Otto didn't take his eyes off Mena and she suddenly looked up at him: "So many after it. Poor thing hadn't a chance."

" ' Bout as much chance as the rabbits," said Otto, grinning.

On the bottom, the hunters had recovered the dead wolf and the dogs were fighting and circling again. The line reformed and moved on toward the tracks, but everyone felt that the greatest excitement had passed. Otto was aware of his weary legs and Mena's feet dragged. She kicked up a rabbit but didn't fire—Ira brought it down.

"You didn't shoot on purpose," accused Otto.

"Couldn't get my mitten off," she explained, but color that wasn't wind-made came into her face.

They came to a small tributary of the river, its banks thick with willows and cottonwoods, and Ira pointed to a nest high up: "I see some fur up there."

Harry yelled: "Squirrel. Let him have it."

Ira's shot sent leaves and twigs flying from the nest. A side of sandy fur showed on the edge; then a black face appeared, hesitant, dazed, injured. " 'Coon," yelled Otto. They stared astonished as the animal tottered high above them in the old crow's nest; then toppled over and came crashing through the branches. Ira ran to the base of the tree and held high the dead raccoon by its ringed tail.

They gathered around him admiring it.

"That'll make a fine pelt," Wallace said. "Worth money now all these college kids are wearin' 'coonskin coats." Then he added: "Fine roast too. Ever eat roast 'coon?"

A new excitement hit them. "We'll get Mom to roast it," said Harry.

"I could stand a bite right now," put in Ira.

"Go ahead," said Otto. "I'll watch." They laughed.

The railroad tracks were getting closer now and they stumbled on toward the embankment and flung themselves down upon it. "Boy, am I tired," gasped Otto. Mena and Ira were too all-in to talk.

Then Ed Crosby came along the tracks looking for them. They let him carry their bags and guns to the car. Only Harry seemed less weary.

"Suppose Ma'll roast Ira's 'coon, Dad?" he said, climbing into the front seat.

"Sure," said his father.

Then Harry turned to the others: "Hey, kids, this's better'n goin' to school."

He got no reply. All three had tumbled into the back seat. Ira had crumpled into one corner; Otto and Mena were curled up together, dead to the world.

"Sissies," Harry grunted in disgust.

Ed looked back at them—his eyes rested a moment on Mena and Otto; then with a chuckle, he started the car and drove home.

AUTHOR (LEFT) AND A NEIGHBOR IN
FAMILY APPLE ORCHARD, 1913 OR 1914.

❧ ❧ Clarence Andrews

CLARENCE ANDREWS was born in Waterloo in 1912 and was raised (Iowans are "raised," not "reared") in Cedar Rapids where he graduated from high school in 1930. For the next nineteen years, somehow suppressing a lifelong urge to write, he worked as an office machine salesman and mechanic in Cedar Rapids, Sioux City, Mason City, Ottumwa, and Sheldon. In 1949, over the protests of his wife and three children, he took the advice of a friend and advantage of the GI bill and enrolled as a freshman in Sheldon Junior College. The following year he enrolled at the University of Iowa because of the reputation of Paul Engle's Iowa Writers' Workshop. He was awarded the Ph.D. from Iowa in 1963.

In the years since 1949 he has published pulp fiction (in such magazines as *Dime Detective*) and humor, a great many classified technical documents, five books, and numerous articles in newspapers, magazines, and journals. He has also, since 1958, "moonlighted" as a teacher in order to support his writing efforts. For some of those years he lived in Arizona and the Upper Peninsula of Michigan, but most of his life has been in Iowa.

The title of this piece, "Did You Ever See a Dream Walking—?" (1976), comes from one of the musical comedies of the 1930s, probably one of the screen musicals that featured Ruby Keeler and Dick Powell. Andrews has always been a theatrical and film buff. Here he recounts some of that aspect of his life.

DID YOU EVER
SEE A DREAM WALKING—?

A THEATER "COMP" was my golden spoon, the "Clink" my prep school, the Isis my country club. My moral behavior was not so much conditioned by memorizing the titles of the books of the Old and New Testaments forwards and backwards as it was by the sure-as-hard-times certainty that the good guys would triumph over the bad guys; that William Powell, the crooked governor, or Clark Gable, accomplice in guilt with Jean Harlow, would stand before a tribunal of their peers at the end of the picture and confess the errors of their ways; and that feminine purity would be defended.

The often grim realities of growing up in an Iowa workingman's home, of living across the street from the Williams and Hunting mill just two blocks from the stink of the starch works or in the shantytown of "Time Check," were made easier by the hours spent in the Palace, the Strand, the Olympia, the Rialto, the Capitol, the Columbia, the Paramount, the Grand, the Majestic, the Bijou, transported by the larger-than-life seductive fantasies created by the shadows on the silver screen or actors on a stage. There I could forget that my mother and father were at home packing their meager household goods in preparation for another move to another coldwater shack because once more the rent was overdue and the landlord was pounding at the door.

My education in escaping from reality into fantasy began even before my formal education in one public school after another in Waterloo and Cedar Rapids. It began in a theater on the bank of the Red Cedar River on West Fourth Street. I was three or four then and I got my first crush on an actress. One scene sticks in my mind. L. Lucille LaValliere is sitting at a table, virginal in her white evening gown and encrusted with diamonds and pearls. The oily villain, slick and black in his tuxedo and patent leather slippers, leers at her from under his varnished black hair with the crease in the middle. "Who did your portrait there?" he asks, pointing to the canvas wall behind her. As she turns to look before giving him her answer, the sly rogue empties a vial into her wine glass. A moment later she is unconscious and he is helping himself to the jewels.

But as vivid as that scene is the memory of coming out of the Waterloo playhouse balcony onto a rickety spiderweb of a fire escape with the black waters far below reflecting the lights of the Fifth Street bridge. The chasm loomed like death and I cried and screamed to be taken back into the dark sanctuary of the building where L. Lucille was. But we made our way safely down into the streets. And all the way out to East John Street where we lived in a two-room house on the bank of Virden Creek, I sat with my visions of a world beyond the reality of death and the East Fourth Street trolley.

My mother never had any use for the theater, films, radio, television, or any form of escape from the harsh Puritan reality she had been raised in. We went to the theater because my father wanted to go. He had come to enjoy these cheap tastes of what the theater could be because before his marriage, before my coming, he had worked as a stagehand at the old Greene's Opera House in Cedar Rapids.

Some of my later childhood memories are of his winter tales of backstage make-believe. He told of the perennial *Uncle Tom's Cabin* and that indelible scene in which Liza leaps from the frigid bank of the Ohio onto the ice cakes below as Haley, the trader, comes up behind with a pack of baying bloodhounds. The bloodhounds, a dramatic innovation in the play, had been borrowed from the coal yard of the W. G. Block Company, where on other nights they stood guard duty against those who would raid the yard in the dark. The stage water, although not frigid, was genuine water and the ice floe was made up of large blocks of wood painted white. The scene was so real that even in the warm womb of the darkened auditorium the audience shivered.

But the grandest tale of all was the account of the climactic scene in *Ben Hur*—the chariot race between Ben Hur and Messala, once his boyhood friend, now his bitterest enemy. The Roman Colosseum was simulated by a revolving endless panorama of painted canvas circling on two poles, one at each side of the stage. Against this moving backdrop, enlivened by stagehands and boys from the street making crowd noises backstage, two genuine chariots, each "pulled" by two live (and very lively) horses, thundered and bounced, their wheels spinning on the slats of treadmills set on the stage for this purpose. The treadmills themselves were on wheels with a rope at each end so that stagehands offstage could tug them back and forth to give the sense that now Ben Hur's chariot was ahead, now Messala's.

"My job was to pull on the rope that was tied to Ben Hur's chariot," my father would say. While my mother glared at him, we would shiver in vicarious delight at his identification with one of the good guys. "As the race came to an end, the horse's mouth was within inches of my face and I could feel the hot spray spitting from his lips. One misstep, one broken slat in the treadmill, and horse, chariot, actor, and I would have gone through the wall and out into the alley!"

You see that my memories of growing up in Iowa are of fantasies, of

"The often grim realities of growing up in an Iowa working-man's home . . . were made easier by the hours spent in the Palace, the Strand, the Olympia, the Rialto, the Capitol, the Columbia, the Paramount, the Grand, the Majestic, the Bijou . . ."

Second Avenue, looking West, Cedar Rapids, Iowa.

dreams walking on a stage, of silvery shadows on a piece of cloth stretched across a wall. And sometimes I wonder if the memories themselves are not fantasies—was it in Waterloo or in Cedar Rapids or nowhere that Tricky Dicky slipped the Mickey to L. Lucille?

A couple of years back, up in Michigan's Northern Peninsula, I was conducting a call-in radio show and talking with elderly people who were recalling a tragedy sixty years before where some seventy people, mostly children, died as they stampeded out of a second-floor auditorium. After the show a former resident of Cedar Rapids who now lives in the Upper Peninsula telephoned me. "How much do you remember of the 1919 starch works explosion?" he demanded. "Quite a bit," I said. "I can still hear the noise, see the dark cloud of smoke in the sky." He interrupted: "Do you actually recall the explosion—or what you read and were told in the years afterward?"

His point, I suppose, is a good one. But regardless of the source, I still have memories of growing up in a world of fantasies: the L. Lucille LaVallieres of the traveling troupes, the Neil Hamiltons and Jason Robards of the Hollywood dream factories, Toby plays in canvas tents parked on the old circus grounds, J. Doug Morgan's company at the Majestic.

That fantasy world—a world of purely good and purely evil, a concept in itself a fantasy as we have come to learn—was easily defined. The women were good even though not always gowned in virginal white satin. Even the fallen women turned out to have hearts of gold, although they often died for their earlier trespasses. The good guys were easily identified even though they did not always wear white or ride a white horse as Tom Mix did. We knew from the beginning on which side of law and order Mix, Hoot Gibson, Bob Steele, Buck Jones, Bill Hart, Harry Carey, or Rin Tin Tin would be. And we knew that even though they were in serious trouble in the beginning, seemingly pitted against overwhelming Evil (his face was familiar!), they would win out in the end.

And in serious cases the Cavalry could always be depended on to come charging over the brow of the hill, bugles sounding "Charge!" the Stars and Stripes a-flying!

(Only once did Hollywood let us down on that score. Bob Steele rode to the cavalry outpost to report that the Indians were massacring the whites—but found only a lone sentry there! Years later we learned that the film was made on a shoestring and the film company had spent all its money for extras when it hired the Indians!)

Tom Mix, the trickster, usually had only his wonder horse Tony, his rope, and his wits—he rarely used violence. In some cases Tony would carry a message or go for help. In others he would help Mix untie the Western's equivalent of the Gordian knot. Most often, Mix did the job himself. There was the film where all the bad guys and the fallen women (their legs showed!) were having an orgy in a second-floor dance hall. With a hammer and saw, Mix quickly converted the outdoor stairway to a slide and he lassooed each villain who slid unexpectedly on his derriere to the ground. In another film Mix hired a local band to march seven times around the dance hall, playing loudly. On the seventh lap, the building fell down! The moral was obvious: stay away from dance halls and fallen women and keep your wits about you.

My earliest memory of a motion picture is not of the picture itself but of the theater—the old Strand in Cedar Rapids. The picture was *Forbidden Fruit* (and that's no fantasy—I looked it up). To con the guileless into attending, the underside of the marquee was trimmed with actual pieces of fruit: apples, bananas, pineapples. My father, a tall man, was egged on by those around him to help himself to one of the pieces of ''forbidden fruit'' and he did. And not even an usher came over to reprimand him!

From my later reading of Gen. 1 and 2, and my frequent attendance at a great many movies, I'll wager that *Forbidden Fruit* had a snake attired in a black tuxedo, patent leather slippers and varnished hair. I'll also wager, knowing both the original tale and the movies, that there was a fallen woman or two around. My final bet is that those attending saw only the temptation and not the Fall!

By and large the masculine gang of my youth did not go for such exotic examples of the filmmakers' craft. We disdained for the most part what we called ''society'' films—movies whose performers spent all their time in white shirts, black suits, long dresses, and patent leather slippers. We were a blue jeans crowd, partly by choice and partly for economic reasons. However, I gazed longingly more than once at the cowboy suits for boys offered for sale in the Killian toy department, and all of us dug through the trash cans of the Harper Auto Works looking for bits of canvas, leatherette, and shiny metal buttons to make us look like our idols of the silver screen.

Our film fare was whatever cowboy movie the ''Clink'' (its formal name was the Colonial) showed on a Saturday afternoon. Our heroes were Tom Mix, Hoot Gibson, Harry Carey, and William S. Hart, in about that order. On the lighter side, any comedy featuring Harold Lloyd (who can ever forget *Safety Last?*), Fatty Arbuckle (until his Fall), Our Gang, or Charlie Chase. Buster Keaton was a bit too artsy-crafty for us, and Charlie Chaplin was all right as long as Jackie Coogan was somewhere in the offing.

Our Gang was Swede, Nelly, Kenny, Floyd, Gar, and I plus any occasional stragglers who would agree to play the heavies—the cowboys in the black suits or the unfriendly Indians. Every film we saw was acted out afterward in and around the sidehill, three-story barn in which Nelly Nelson's father (one of the town's ragpickers) kept his nag. The barn was ideal for our purpose because it had two entrances: one on the ground floor on the river side (where the nag was stabled), one on the second floor on the uphill side where the wagon was kept. An interior ladder led to the hayloft on the third floor and a stairway led down to the stable.

The third floor figured prominently in our reenactments. It had three exits: the ladder, the window through which the hay was lofted, and a chute in the corner down which the hay was pitched to the hungry horse in his first-floor stable. If Swede, for instance, were chased up the ladder he could hang out the hay window and drop four or five feet. But if Kenny had that route cut off, the only other option to being tumbled in the hay was a fifteen-to-twenty foot drop down that chute. Only the foolhardy attempted that unless someone with foresight had pitched some hay down. Then there was only the problem of the hungry horse.

Before any action could begin we had to assign roles, which we usually did, using a ball bat or a broomstick and the method we used to determine who got first choice when we "chose up sides" for a ball game. The bat or stick was tossed in the air and one of the two acknowledged leaders (usually Nelly or Swede) grabbed it and formed a fist around the base. The other then formed a fist around the stick just above, close to the first fist. The first person then placed the fist of his other hand above the second fist. Fist by fist the two worked their way up the stick until no room was left at its top end. The owner of the last fist got first choice. Nelly, tall, blonde, identified easily with Hoot Gibson and usually chose to be the comic Hoot. Swede, always sentimental, would opt for the sentimental Carey (if any of the Western heroes died at the end of the film or before, it was likely to be Carey). The dark, short Kenny Fox, who moved away from our neighborhood after his mother's tragic death from cancer, usually got the fat part of the trickster, Mix. The nag became Tony, the wonder horse, if he was not out pulling the wagon. That left the stern-faced Hart up for grabs with none of the rest of us really grabbing; Hart, like Keaton, was a bit too intellectual for us. Moreover, also like Keaton, he seldom smiled.

Our horses were broomsticks, thrust between our legs, with a rope or heavy cord tied to the upper end for reins. Our guns were made from y-shaped tree branches, one part of the tripod the barrel, another part the handle, the third part the hammer. I still recall the traumatic state produced in me when Miss Roach, our second-grade teacher at Taylor School, caught me in the act of gunning down one of the other cowboys with an elm branch and made me reproduce the action the next day in the classroom. Her intentions were undoubtedly good but the transfer of our fantastic imitation of the screen fantasy into the reality of the classroom and the jeers of my classmates were more than I could endure. In an uncowboylike bit of behavior, I fled from the room in tears and it took a stern edict from Estella Swem, the principal, to get me back.

The Clink, a west-side neighborhood movie house only a block away on Third Avenue, was run by the Naso family who owned the fruit store next door. The Nasos lived in the back of the store and various members of the family happily pocketed our dimes, whether they were tendered for fruit, candy, ice cream, or theater seats. We watched every Western and every comedy in the thick of incongruous fruity aromas that either seeped through the walls or were carried in on the persons of the several Nasos, who somehow managed to operate both enterprises at once.

We speculated long and loudly during the duller moments of the silent films about the magical technology that produced them. My position was that a group of midgets or dwarves spent their evenings and Saturday and Sunday afternoons in the basement beneath the stage of the Clink, pushing huge pictures up into our view. My occasional visits to the rest room underneath the stage (which had an odor quite unlike that of the fruit store) were lengthened as I sought for the door that undoubtedly led to that workshop. And then one afternoon in the alley behind the Clink, I found a strip of positive film. Held up to the light, it revealed scenes in miniature from the Mix movie of the previous Saturday. I treasured that bit of reality for a long time.

Yet even an inspection of the bit of film did not entirely clear up the mystery of film technology. We could not put together the man crawling up into the tiny loft at the rear of the Clink, the piece of film, and the beam of light flickering through the small round opening in the rear wall. We could no more understand how these phenomena produced a larger-than-life image of a galloping horse on the screen than we could understand certain unmentionable mysteries of the origins of life.

But we could understand what took place on the screen. We knew immediately who the good guys were and who the bad guys were, we knew that the good guys would be in a precarious and worsening situation at the beginning, we knew that they would triumph at the end. And we waited expectantly for the end for we knew that it would bring either the excitement of the chase or of the battle-to-the-death on the edge of a cliff.

But as we learned much later in life, we overestimated our understanding. We could not know that the bad guys could symbolize the fear of death hanging over our heads and the chase and the battle could represent man's triumph over death. Nor, because the films simplified the matter of good and evil (usually making of them a morality play), could we understand that the films did not attempt to deal with the complexities of good and evil, that the villain, unlike his counterparts in real life, had no sympathetic psychologist or sociologist to try to understand his problems or Constitution to guarantee his right to a trial before his peers. Nor, ultimately, could we see that the poetic justice that led to his demise had no real counterpart in life, either in the criminal courts or out of them. We enjoyed the uncomplicated endings because we wanted life to be simpler than we were learning it was as we grew up. A dead Indian was a good Indian, and a dead bad guy was a good bad guy.

Then one Saturday afternoon at the Clink, we began to expand our outlook on the world. Africa! To ensure that we would be there with our dimes the next fifteen Saturday afternoons, the Nasos showed the first episode of a fifteen-episode serial set in Africa. The old morality of white as good and black as evil carried on; the white hero and his girl were constantly being pursued by black-skinned people. But this was somewhat more complex; the blacks were usually led by an evil white man named Caja, and Caja promptly became the newest villain in our games. Had we gone but two blocks away, over on H Street along the river toward the starch works, we could have found genuine black-skinned people to play their counterparts. But we knew better than to go looking for trouble of that kind.

Each episode ended with the hero or the girl or both in peril of their hides. The hero might be swinging, a human pendulum, over a slough full of hungry alligators, with his time becoming shorter with every swing. Or the girl might be pursued by a horde of blacks throwing their spears with ever more deadly aim at her back. Or the hero would be bound, ready to be thrown into a pit of hungry lions, while off to the side Caja was bargaining with a gang of dark-skinned men to sell the girl into a fate worse than death.

Such episodes gave us new adventures to practice. Now we tied a rope to a tree branch and swung out over the waters of the Cedar River. Or we pushed our way through the odoriferous shallows of a dark tunnel that carried a small stream from the country under the west side of town. Here we encountered a fierce beast as dangerous to us as the lion to the screen hero—the sewer rat!

Seeking other means of imitating Africa we pushed our way down the river past the black residential area, past the smelly starch works, to Riverside Park. Here were horizontal ladders to swing on as we made our way from "tree" to "tree." Here were rope swings and slides and tall metal supports to shinny up and slide down.

Fifteen Saturday afternoons passed and Caja and his black horde got their just deserts. The "manifest destiny" of the white race triumphed again!

But on that final Saturday afternoon, Mr. Naso laid a new trap for us and our dimes and set a new challenge to our imaginations. Within seconds after Caja had gasped his last, we were introduced to the brunette Ruth Roland, Queen of the Western serials. At the moment in that first episode when Ruth met the Man, the pianist in the orchestra pit of the Clink began playing "Whispering,"

Whispering while I cuddle near you . . .

and L. Lucille LaValliere took second place in my fantasies! In the course of the next fifteen Saturday afternoons, Ruth and the song and the fruity aroma would be indelibly joined in my memories. Even today, to hear "Whispering" (or even the odor of a fruit salad!) evokes sweet memories of Ruth.

Thereafter Africa was forgotten and we were once again in the wild, wild West. We began scouring First Street West and Fourth and Fifth avenues for a brunette girl. We found one or two but they preferred to play "house" or "doctor," and so, unwillingly, I became Ruth Roland!

But I came to like the part. Now I could hang by my fingertips from the third-floor edge of the hay chute in imitation of Ruth at the end of Episode 3. Now I could slide from a rope tied to a hook in the barn's attic. And one memorable day I made my way to the roof of the barn, carrying the huge striped canvas umbrella that Mr. Nelson shaded himself with on sunny days. At the edge of the roof I opened the umbrella and, using it as a parachute, floated down to the ground in imitation of Ruth's daring "dive to death" from the wing tip of a canvas biplane!

It was ever so much more exciting to do real things like that than it was to run up and down through the barn yelling, "Bang, bang, you're dead," at some bigger boy who refused to lie down!

When I was eight (the year was 1920), I began selling newspapers for Alex Fidler, the *Cedar Rapids Gazette* street circulation manager, and as a fringe benefit, learned of the magic of the theater "comp." Now I could go over town to the Palace, the Isis, the Majestic, the Strand, the Rialto. This free ticket was a privilege other members of the gang did not have and I became somewhat of a hero in their eyes. For my comp allowed me to take one friend with me.

Swede, my younger brother, was only six or seven at the time, and my mother (her feeling about the theatrical world has already been mentioned) would not allow him to go with me. But one summer night she wanted to go to the hospital to see my sick father, so she said I might take him along provided we stayed only through one show. (She knew only too well how much the films fascinated me.)

We were living out on Ellis Boulevard then, a long walk to town and a long walk home. As soon as we were away from the house I proposed to Swede that we cut over to Sixth Street and "hook" an Ellis Park streetcar bound for town. It would be easy, I argued; the car had a "cowcatcher" (a wire basket of sorts) attached to each end and it was always left in its down position. Besides, how many times had I seen Ruth Roland "hook" onto a plane, a train, a trolley, an automobile.

We were still debating the propriety of such an act when the car came upon us from behind and stopped at the corner just ahead to take on a passenger. Now was our chance. If we got the car, we could be over town that much sooner and see that much more of the movie. I grabbed Swede by the hand and began running. But even then he was taller than I and he made it to the car just as it began to move. He jumped onto the cowcatcher but my short legs defeated me and I was left behind.

It did not occur to either Swede or me then what Ruth Roland would have done in such a predicament. But halfway down the block, Swede made up his mind—he jumped from the moving car into the street and went tumbling and rolling over the ties.

He was screaming with pain when I got to him. He wanted to go home, but I wanted to see the film. Moreover, there was no point in going home because no one was there. So on we went. All the way to the Palace, all through the film, all the way home he sobbed with pain.

We were in for it, we knew, if we told my mother the truth. The comp would be torn up and there would be no more movies.

That night we watched Episode 14 of a Ruth Roland serial. At the end of the episode, Ruth and her lover had been trapped in a van by the scheming villain, and the van had been pushed off a dock into very deep water. Slowly, slowly the water rose in the van, to their knees, to their waists, to their chins. Scarcely three inches of airspace was left in the van. The camera moved outside, and horrified, we watched the van slowly sink into the watery depths. The pianist had long since ceased to play "Whispering."

I just had to see the final episode of that serial the following week, so we concocted the most plausible lie we could. It had nothing to do with hooking a ride on a streetcar or any kind of behavior for which we could be punished. If either Tom Mix or Ruth Roland had been standing in the room as we told my mother that Swede had stumbled over a steep curb on a dark street corner, they would have blushed.

But at the moment my mother had little time for interrogation. It turned out that Swede had a broken collarbone and he was rushed off to the hospital at once. Morning found him in the bed next to my father.

The week passed. Swede and my father both came home, each much improved. No more questions were asked about the accident. As much as possible I avoided both parents. And the night for the showing of the fifteenth episode arrived.

Clutching my comp in my hand I hurried over town to the Palace. I deliberately avoided Sixth Street and the Ellis Park trolley line.

There was a long line outside the entrance to the Palace. They were showing a Douglas Fairbanks film, and I learned later the film had been sold out for every performance. In order to accommodate all who were trying to get in to see the film, the management had canceled all the performance except the feature.

The usher refused to admit me when I finally came to the door. He pointed to a sign stating that all comps were canceled for that show.

"But I want to see Chapter 15 of the serial," I said.

"We're not showing the serial," he said. "Only the feature."

"When will you show Chapter 15?" I asked. "Next week?"

"Next week we start a new serial," he said. "Now beat it, kid."

Right then, and for a long time afterward, I was sure that the poetic justice of the films was working in my case. I had lied and I was being punished for my crime.

The years have passed, a great many of them. My love affair with the theater, with the stage, with the movies, has never ended. I may never see as many films as that child prodigy, Leonard Maltin, who at eighteen produced a book in which he set out thumbnail sketches of 8,000 films he had seen, but I've seen so many that I can't begin to remember even a small fraction. I'm the one the TV stations run and rerun the old movies for.

But I still wonder just how Ruth Roland got out of that water-filled van.

🌺 🌺 Julie McDonald

STICK A pin anywhere in a map of Iowa and you will pinpoint a part of Iowa's ethnic heritage. Croatians and Italians in Centerville; Middle Eastern Syrians with their Moslem mosque in Cedar Rapids; Bohemians in Iowa City, Cedar Rapids, and Spillville; Norwegians in Decorah; Germans in Hancock County and Davenport; Hungarians in Davenport; Luxemburgers in Gilbertville; blacks in Des Moines; Frisian and Dutch in Pella and northwest Iowa; Mesquakie, Sac and Fox Indians in Tama; Scots at Scotch Grove and the hills of northern Tama County—these are only representative of the varied groups who came to the "beautiful land" in the nineteenth and early twentieth centuries and who settled here to make Iowa the place it is. The names of Iowa cities and towns reflect these ethnic diversities: Dubuque, Wapello, Moravia, Amana, Germantown, Albion, Ayrshire, Scotch Grove, Bettendorf, Bonaparte, Breda, Grafton, Emmetsburg, Holland, Holstein, Luther, Luxemburg, New Vienna, Norway, and many others.

Alone among Iowa novelists (though not among Iowa writers) Julie Jensen McDonald has used the experience of moving from the Old World to the New in *Amalie's Story* (1970), a story of emigration from Denmark to Audubon County, Iowa.

Julie McDonald of Davenport is a well-known Iowa author. Her work includes historical articles about Davenport and Scott County; an *Iowan* article on Floyd Dell, another Iowa author; two back-of-the book novels in *Redbook; Baby Black,* a children's book; and two children's plays, a historical pageant and a two-act comedy. From 1969 to 1973 she was chairwoman of the Iowa Arts Council.

In "Growing Up in Western Iowa" (1976), she looks back at her childhood in the thirties on a farm near now relatively nonexistent Fiscus and in a public school at Harlan. Unlike Phil Stong, Julie McDonald does not see farmhands as jacks-of-all-trades with libraries of books ranging from Voltaire to Twain by way of Kant!

GROWING UP IN WESTERN IOWA

WHEN THE Iowa Department of Transportation removed my native town from the map I was sorry I had done nothing to make Fiscus famous enough to hold its own, but I knew the cartography of my memory would never let it go. Actually, I was born in a farmhouse about a mile east of Fiscus, which makes me a native of Audubon County; that house is gone too, but I remember it well.

Some years ago, having heard that my birthplace was to be torn down, my mother and I made a farewell pilgrimage. The doors were boarded shut to discourage vandals, but my mother had not taken a manual training course at Cedar Falls in the Edwardian years for nothing. She deftly removed the barriers, and we entered the house of my birth for the first time since we left it in my fifth year.

Everything was the same: the pantry to the west, the pass-through from kitchen to dining room, the alcove where my mother kept her sewing machine and where we listened to Eddie Cantor on the radio, the seldom used parlor that once held an old church organ sacrificed for firewood during the depression, the downstairs bedroom where I was born, and the upstairs bedrooms with sloping ceilings where a lazy hired man filled and hid a series of Mason jars rather than make a cold trek to the outhouse. As I walked through the rooms, events and feelings silted over by the years were given back to me.

I was born ten years after my parents were married, and since my mother's frame was suited to the long concealment of pregnancy, many of the neighbors were convinced that I was adopted. I'm told that my infant head was square after an instrument birth, and one of the first visitors to my banana crate crib remarked, "The mold sure was broken when they made that one!"

The hired man of my babyhood had been in and out of what was then called "the Insane Asylum" at Clarinda, and he terrified my mother by lifting me, high chair and all, close to the ceiling. But she was grateful to him for saving my life. I fell from a horse's back and would have been trampled had he not caught the leg of my overalls between two fingers. His name was Jess, and I loved him. They say that Jess whispered things to me, and I responded with a great expression of delight. I wish I knew what

113

he said, but I can't remember. Jess died in that place at Clarinda, with marks on his throat, they said, and it was years before I could believe that Clarinda was a pleasant Iowa town where people lived normal lives.

The farm Christmas I remember best brought me a child-sized table that my father made from an apple box painted bright orange. Two of its legs were made from an old broomstick and the other two were fatter, cut from the round of wood inside a roll of linoleum. And my father made a sack of peanuts in the shell seem as precious as the gifts of the Magi on that happy Christmas.

On Sundays in those depression years, we frequently had company for dinner—people from town who weren't lucky enough to have a yard full of chickens and fattening steers in the feedlot. The minute my mother saw a high, boxy car turn into our lane, she would capture, kill, pluck, and fry a chicken or two in record time.

Otherwise, we had little company but the Watkins man and other salesmen. One of them sold big capsules of a dietary supplement made from alfalfa, and I happily opened them and poured their green contents down the hollow tongue of my little red wagon until I was observed and restrained.

My mother and I sometimes walked to Fiscus, scarcely breathing as we passed the enclosure where a mean bull was kept. We were safe when we reached the Jorgensen Brothers trucking company with its gas pump that looked like a jar of orange soda pop. While my mother shopped at the general store, I sang an obbligato to the monotonous hum of the grain mill next door. The storekeeper always gave me lollipops, which I did not value at the time.

Errands finished, we would visit my Aunt Elsie and Uncle Martin Jensen (he was no relation to my father), whose farm bordered Fiscus. Beating away the flies that clustered on the back screen, we would go inside for a piece of Aunt Elsie's famous burnt sugar cake and some lemonade, and while the sisters talked, I would ''play'' the piano in the parlor or conjure up fantastic beasts from the whorls of the birds-eye maple bedroom furniture.

I saw other children only at Merrill's Grove Baptist Church or at Ladies' Aid meetings in other farm homes. Mostly I amused myself by making tiny paper carts for box-elder bugs to pull with sewing thread, digging trenches with my dog Shep, and brooding about where I ended and infinity began or vice versa.

I learned to lie quite on my own. We had a new rat terrier puppy, and I was barefoot when I carried him along the roadside in front of our house. The weeds in the ditch had been burned out; the gray ashes looked cool enough but the hidden coals burned my feet. Startled, I dropped the pup, and my father, who was cutting branches in the yard, vaulted the fence to rescue the yelping dog. My story was the instant invention that a strange

"I hadn't realized that he was coming."

JULIE, FIVE, AND BROTHER FREDDIE, EIGHT MONTHS.

man came down the road and dropped the dog on the coals. Since my father had seen the whole thing, I got the whipping of my life and was further punished by the sight of the pup lying on his back in a shoe box, his burned paws greased with unsalted butter.

Not that I was without formal moral training. Merrill's Grove Church scheduled its worship service before Sunday school, and when I grew restless during a long sermon, my mother would slip me an oyster cracker, much to the disapproval of Christians sitting near us. I knew about "the little Lord Jesus," but the Devil was more dramatic. Once when Shep threw himself against the snow-covered back door, I was convinced that the huge, dark shape was the Devil himself, and I was a model child for a brief interval.

Our life on the farm moved with the slow cycle of the land and we thought it always would, but change was on the way. Trying to solve a drainage problem, my father dug a ditch, and erosion did its insidious work until a bridge was necessary. My father's team of mules negotiated the bridge without difficulty, but they were cussed beasts, given to stomping kittens to death for fun, and he couldn't have handled them at all if he hadn't learned the knack in the American army in World War I. He was pleased to exchange them for a John Deere tractor, and we all cheered when the mules went down the lane for the last time. The new tractor reminded me of a giant grasshopper.

One morning in April—it was Friday the thirteenth—my mother was reading "Andy Gump" to me when a neighbor came to the gate and shouted for her to come quickly. She left me alone, which was unusual, and when she came back she was sobbing aloud, which was incredible. I can't remember who told me that my father was dead. The funeral home people came from town with a big wicker basket and took him from the ditch where he had fallen beneath the tractor when the bridge collapsed. Shep kept vigil on the bank until they took him away.

I saw my father for the last time in the funeral home, lying in bed in his Sunday suit with a pink jacquard bedspread pulled to his waist. He wore the wedding ring that was too dangerous for a working farmer. Unnatural. I was not allowed to attend the funeral, but I heard that the church was packed. My father, who came to this country from Denmark when he was nineteen, was an avid reader and Bible student. Those who knew the play of his mind spoke admiringly of it, but how could a four-year-old appreciate such riches? To no avail, I asked God to give him back.

About four months later, I started to country school, carrying my lunch bucket a mile to listen to the seriatim instruction of eight grades and to drink from the common water dipper. The long-established custom of harassing the beginning class was an unpleasant revelation to me, and at first I tried to buy my way out of the abuse by bringing a tractor umbrella the older kids needed for a project. No one at our house seemed to care what happened to the tractor or any of its accessories. The older kids took my umbrella and clobbered me.

Thereafter, I started out for school each morning as usual, but I spent the day with a kind farmwife who did not betray me, and when I saw the others going home from school, I went home too. This routine lasted for two weeks, but when I saw the teacher's Model T Ford turn into our lane, I knew the jig was up and ran to lock myself in the outhouse.

My country school experience lasted only twenty days, including the ten I was absent, and then we moved to Harlan to live with my Grandma Faurschou in her little gray house on Willow Street. Accustomed to night silence in the country broken only by the occasional howling of winter wolves, I was startled by train whistles in town and expected the locomotive to rush down the street past the house.

And that wasn't the only adjustment I had to make. At first, I was put into first grade at Laurel School, but I was nearly a year younger than the others, and I soon was sent back to kindergarten for reasons of "social adjustment."

Social adjustment wasn't easy in kindergarten. Scorning a beautiful naptime rug hand-hooked by my grandmother, I wanted one from the dime store to be like everyone else. I was ridiculed for coloring a tree trunk black because I didn't have a brown crayon, and the class beauty said, "You have *lines* in your hand!" Her own pudgy palm was as smooth as butter.

One of the most exciting events at Grandma's house was the midnight collapse of the bed slats. I hung suspended in a featherbed shaped like an oriole's nest and enjoyed it hugely. Another memorable awakening occurred early in a cold November day when Grandma told me I had a baby brother. He was born seven months after my father's death, and in all the grief and confusion, I hadn't realized that he was coming. That Christmas we had a tree lit by candles clamped to the branches with fish-shaped holders. A full bucket of water stood next to the tree for safety's sake.

The next Christmas, when I was six, I walked through the streets with my mother, admiring holiday lights, with an incipient case of chicken pox. I caught a chill and began a cycle of ill health that was to persist for years and cause me to substitute books for belly whoppers on a sled or any other active childhood pastime.

My mother sold the Ford she had taught herself to drive on the farm, once ramming a haystack when she couldn't figure out how to stop it, and she bought a house on Tenth Street across from my Aunt Mary and Uncle Clarence Jacobsen. It was here that I got really sick with mastoiditis and complications that called for two operations and five weeks in Jennie Edmundson Hospital, Council Bluffs. The surgeons gave me a chance in a thousand to live, but after six blood transfusions from a Holy Roller, I made it. This was the winter of 1936, when the Dionne quintuplets were the darlings of the globe, when "The Music Goes Round and Round" was heard incessantly, and when Mother Nature did her worst. My mother froze her knees walking from a rooming house to the hospital to see me.

The society of my childhood was anything but pluralistic. St. Michael's Catholic Church, built in Spanish mission style, was just north of my grade school, and sometimes I sneaked into the vestibule to snatch a glance at its dark mysteries. I liked the statues and the candles, and I wanted to stick a finger into the holy water font but was afraid. Of Judaism I knew nothing. Sometimes I took care of two little Jewish girls while their parents worked at the grocery, and I learned to recognize a matzo ball but nothing else. Added to these mysteries was the matter of color. We had no blacks in Harlan, and on rare excursions to Omaha, I would stare at black faces with awe.

Before we embraced the uplifting activities of Girl Scouting, my friends and I amused ourselves by making time capsules. Filling a Karo syrup can with newspaper stories (among them an account of Errol Flynn's indictment for rape, which we didn't understand because our elders would not define the word and we couldn't believe that anything unmentionable would be included in the dictionary) and documentation of our own identities, we begged fresh cement from a sidewalk project and sealed our capsule. Buried in the bank behind Joyce McGowan's house on Tenth Street, it has never come to light as far as I know. Other messages to posterity may be found on the lathes of our house at Ninth and Willow streets, inserted by small hands through the openings for sliding double doors.

Milk was not delivered to our house. Each night, I carried an empty tin pail with a lid to a dairy within the city limits and brought it back full. The milk was unpasteurized and thick, yellow cream rose to the top. I never performed this errand with dispatch. When the bail started to cut my palm, I would set the bucket down and climb a tree to watch the sunset and think about life in general. In warm weather, I overshot the dairy to wade in the creek that ran through a pasture. The telltale bubbles of a hidden crawdad prompted the search for a tin can to carry the creature home.

Though we didn't own a piano, I took lessons from Miss May Davis, a true gentlewoman, and practiced at Aunt Mary's house. My mother's sister sat on the bench beside me and counted. When the practice session was over, she discoursed on the Good, the True, and the Beautiful. Her daughter, my cousin Marjorie, was a near virtuoso, and I suppose that discouraged me. I abandoned the piano for the clarinet (though I really wanted to play the flute), starting on a metal instrument that was school property when I was in fourth grade.

Play an instrument and see the world! At the age of ten, I was in

Kansas City at a regional music contest. My mother always plaited the braids that fell below my waist, and without her, I went uncombed for three days. But even after such a thrilling reward for effort, I hated to practice. When I moved the clock hands with my fingers to make the terrible hour go faster, I was apprehended and punished. Music at least taught me a discipline valuable to a writer, and in time, it gave me pleasure—especially after I received an excellent instrument, which I still use, for my eleventh birthday.

When I was in the sixth grade, an indulgent teacher, Miss Carolyn Kahler, allowed the class to produce a play I had written, "The Whispering Mummy." By this time, we had moved into a big, old house at the corner of Ninth and Willow streets, and the former owners left a huge library behind, including a number of books by Sax Rohmer, the creator of Dr. Fu Manchu. Inspired by Rohmer, I created a play of such violent suspense (for me, at least) that I forgot the lines I had written for myself.

When Grandma moved out of her Willow Street house into ours, I was scarcely needed for household tasks, but they were still assigned for the purpose of character building. I soon learned that a book in the hand was a sure defense against chores. Reading was a nearly holy activity that must not be interrupted.

Armed with this knowledge, I made frequent trips to the Carnegie Library and chewed through all the fairy tales on the shelves. A big tree on the library lawn dropped rich, brown buckeyes that I longed to collect, but the "Keep Off the Grass" sign held me back. Other prohibitions had less effect. Tender young maidens were forbidden to read Lillian Smith's

"I got really sick with mastoiditis. . . . The surgeons gave me a chance in a thousand to live."

JULIE, AGE SIX, IN FRONT OF
JENNIE EDMUNDSON MEMORIAL HOSPITAL.

Strange Fruit, then, quaint as it now seems, considered to be a dirty book. Hidden in the stacks, I read it bit by bit, marking my place with a long hair from my head when I heard someone approaching. Miss Minnie Brazee, the diminutive librarian with gold-rimmed glasses and a whisper with the impact of a shout, never knew of my depravity—as far as I know. My only regret about that library is that I wandered too soon from the sunny southern half of the reading room where the children's books were kept to the darker northern half, where I chose adult books beyond my ken and ruined my desire to return to them for a very long time.

Church activities took up a good portion of my young life: Sunday school, morning worship, youth group, and evening services on Sunday; prayer meeting on Wednesday; choir practice on Thursday; and bulletin mimeographing on Saturday. I spent a good deal of time beneath the reproachful gaze of a lighted, sentimental Jesus at the front of the Bethel Baptist sanctuary, and the bar of Palmolive soap in the women's rest room exuded what I took for the odor of sanctity. From the time when I carried pennies tied in a corner of my handkerchief to Sunday school until long after the night I carried home a long-stemmed red rose after my winter baptism by immersion, I tried unsuccessfully to make that lithographed Jesus look happier, and I was much relieved when I encountered other artists' conceptions of the Christ.

Bethel Baptist Church was strict in all matters of faith and practice, and I was scandalized weekly when I walked home from church and passed the Lutherans smoking nonchalantly on their own church lawn. Movies were on the moral borderline, but I did go to the Harlan Theater on the rare occasions when I had a dime for admission. I sat through *Jane Eyre* three times because I was in love with Orson Welles. Then it was Paul Henreid in something with Bette Davis and Tyrone Power in *Blood and Sand.*

My friends and I collected pictures of movie stars, trading something like two Betty Grables for one Lana Turner; and since nobody shared my intense interest in Hedy Lamarr, I had a magnificent collection of her photographs, including a still of the famous nude scene in *Ecstasy*. In our Hollywood phase, we wore green fingernail polish in total ignorance of Sally Bowles and sent coupons for free samples of anything to make us beautiful.

I was forbidden to go to the roller skating rink because my mother disapproved of the crowd there, and the drugstore soda fountains seldom saw me because I had no money. My generous best friend, Shirley Plumb, got an allowance big enough for two, but I had my pride. The rare cherry coke consumed in the heady, medicinal atmosphere at Pexton's, Norgaard's, or Levendahl's was a peerless treat, and the occasion was enhanced by prolonged mooning in front of the cobalt blue gift sets of Evening in Paris.

Briefly, I had a surefire source of income—baby-sitting for ten cents an hour—but I was dismissed for telling frightening bedtime stories. Actually, they were *Arabian Nights* tales freely adapted, and the kids loved them, nightmares notwithstanding.

My junior high school teachers live strongly in my memory. First there was Anna Carmichael, who wrote the grammar text she taught and made all the rules seem as natural as breathing. I doubt that anyone who saw it will ever forget the time Miss Carmichael clutched the blond hair of Tiny Lund (the late stock car racer) and banged his head on the desk until his nose bled, to get his attention, I think. Then there was Lily Knox, who taught literature and etched "Invictus" on my mind, whether I agreed with its theme or not. And Jessie Myers, the arithmetic teacher, who could have taught me that discipline if anyone could, but I had a mental block about math. These three women were the perennials, and the annual man who rounded out the faculty made little impression on me. In his room, whoever he was, I sketched the ornate wooden bell tower of the Christian church across the street.

In winter, we heated only the kitchen, and the big cookstove was the source of all life. It cooked the food, dried wet mittens, and with the oven door open, made a bearable bathing place in a big washtub with hot water from the reservoir and several teakettles. Toast was browned and flatirons were heated on the burners and bread rose above the warming ovens. My job was to bring cobs and coal from shed and basement to keep it blazing.

The bathroom was cold but it was better than an outhouse, and we carried hot flatirons wrapped in tea towels to bed with us to warm our feet in the icy bedrooms. Sleeping under layers of heavy, homemade quilts, we awoke aching from the weight of the covers. When we wanted to listen to "One Man's Family" or "Jack Benny" on the big radio with its cathedral window speaking screen, we wrapped quilts around us and braved the cold dining room.

Being home sick was not unpleasant. A couch with one end that cranked up like a hospital bed was placed opposite the kitchen stove. A rack of fancy, souvenir plates above it provided a feast for the eye, and the radio could be turned up loud enough to bring "Stella Dallas" from the next room.

Memorial Day, or Decoration Day as my grandmother called it, was a big event in Harlan. For the parade, I put on the awful band uniform of ill-fitting white duck pants, shiny navy twill jacket, and billed cap and played lustily all the way to the cemetery. I was slightly regretful that I didn't know how to faint. Someone else always did, and I would have enjoyed that bit of drama. I had to make do with the terrifying thrill of the rifle salute, tucking my horn under my arm to free my hands for ear covering. And the mausoleum always was unlocked on that day. Morbidly fascinated, we crept inside and mistook the heavy fragrance of peonies for the odor of death.

Actually, I had a sunny relationship with the cemetery. We visited our family graves often. I always entered on the southern drive to pay my respects to a stone angel I admired, but our plot was at the eastern border inside a hedge laced with poison ivy and shaded by a huge pine my grandfather had carried on his shoulder to plant over the grave of my Aunt Laura, dead at thirteen and untimely ripped from a romantically un-consummated love. Now Grandpa Faurschou was under the tree with Laura, and I often wondered how much of them had been drawn into the trunk and branches of the big pine. A short distance to the north was my father, Alfred J. Jensen, and my uncle, Martin Jensen, and there was plenty of room for whoever needed a resting place next.

Since we had no car, Uncle Clarence used to take us for Sunday drives. He was a baseball fan and a chain smoker, and the women in the family dreaded drafts, so the car windows remained shut. Carsick in the back seat, I listened wretchedly to radio baseball entwined with talk like, "The Sorensen girl lives there—she married the Paulsen boy." And the answer, "Oh no, she didn't! She married the youngest Sondergaard, and they live out by Corley."

One summer I worked on a farm doing housework and caring for a small girl. I soon was sent home with the complaint that I ate them out of house and home, to say nothing of pounding out "My Heart at Thy Sweet Voice" on the piano when I should have been dusting.

In time, my voracious appetite was diagnosed as a symptom of a goiter and a raging hyperthyroid condition, unusual in a fourteen-year-old. When I boarded the train for an operation by a Mayo Clinic doctor, I weighed ninety-seven pounds, and when I came home several months later, I weighed one hundred and forty-three and was half dead with humiliation. While my friends were swooning over Frank Sinatra, I was cringing in my mother's clothes. The Rochester experience was interesting, however. I eavesdropped on many lives in the boardinghouse where we stayed before I entered the hospital, and what I didn't hear, I invented for my own amusement. I also tried to make up stories with a sick, fat heroine, but they never seemed to work.

After an absence of several months, I picked up all the courses of my first high school year but Latin. My math block persisted, and if I hadn't been in love with the football coach who taught algebra, I would have failed the course. I did the impossible for him. An English teacher managed to make Caliban and his creator dull, and I did not go back for more for a very long time, but I was reading, always reading.

I played in the city band during the summer, receiving something like five dollars a season, which seemed princely. Sometimes we played on the square near the sad soldier on the Civil War monument, and later we performed at the swimming pool park on a platform strung with yellow bug lights that failed to discourage June bugs. F. D. Curtwright, the conductor, was a decisive man with the baton, and he led us ably through rain, shine, and horse show dust at the fairgrounds.

In my high school years I took a job in a dress shop that involved working Saturday until midnight. This excluded me from the weekly *pasada* around the square, but at least I could look at the passing parade when business was slow. People of all ages walked around the square, which is arranged in the Spanish manner, stopping to talk, shop, or have an ice cream cone. Boys in cars cruised the square, beating on their car doors with their fists at the sight of a youngish female of any description. In spite of my mother's opinion of such folkways, I took secret pleasure in the attention.

By now, I was restless. The permissible was uninteresting, and the forbidden was just that. I could and did read, but I longed for real experience. Petulantly I told my mother, ''The only reason this town exists is that somebody's covered wagon broke down here and they never got it fixed!''

I had never been to Iowa City, but they took me there with most of my worldly goods and settled me into a quonset hut with eight other girls and a proctor. The university caught me up and gave me the view from the top of the Ferris wheel at last.

When I came home that first Christmas, the town had changed. The only thing that stayed the same was the open oven door of the kitchen stove where I curled my toes while I read Thoreau for an English class. When I had warmed myself, I hurried away again.

But I have returned to Harlan again and again to reclaim my childhood. The town may have changed but my feeling for it has not. That first feeling of belonging persists. The house where I was born may be gone and the dot on the map that was Fiscus may go unlabeled, but they are still mine and I now claim the whole of Iowa as fervently as I did that house, that hamlet. From border to border to border, this state is mine!

Richard Lloyd-Jones

JIX LLOYD-JONES is a teacher, a businessman, a poet, a writer, a university administrator, and an important figure in the academic discipline of English composition. In the current furor over Johnnie's and Jennie's inability to write, he has been widely published and publicized. He is presently chair of the Conference on College Composition and Communications, a national organization of college teachers of writing. In the fall of 1976, he was appointed chair of the English Department of the University of Iowa, one of America's better-known English departments. His writing and lecturing are primarily in the discipline of English composition; his audience is largely in that discipline but it is nationwide. His friends who have been privileged recipients of his verse at Christmastime through the years wish that he would write more verse and assemble it in a bound volume.

Jix comes from a distinguished heritage. As he notes in "Fire and Ice: A Rhapsodic View of the 30s" (1976), he springs from the same Welsh roots as Frank Lloyd Wright. A well-known ancestor was Jenkins Lloyd Jones, an educator who helped spread the seeds of liberal thought through Wisconsin and other areas of the Middle West. Another well-known relative, also Jenkins Lloyd Jones, is a nationally syndicated newspaper columnist.

Jean Lloyd-Jones is widely known throughout Iowa and the nation as a prominent member and former president of the League of Women Voters of Iowa.

In this essay Jix looks back at life as a boy in "River City," more formally known as Mason City, the home of several Iowa authors he mentions in his essay.

FIRE AND ICE:
A RHAPSODIC VIEW OF THE 30s

Because you are lukewarm, neither hot nor cold, I will spit you out of my mouth. Rev. 3:16.

THE ICEMAN drove a truck. Hermanson's dairy still used horses and wagons in the 30s in Mason City, and I can recall stuffing the right number of milk tickets in the bottles and putting them out for the driver as he made his dark-of-the-morning rounds. But the iceman rode between the old rural ways and new gadgets. His ice was made at a "factory," not harvested from a pond, and he drove a truck.

We no longer took ice because my father had coils put in our icebox, but some of the neighbors still displayed the cards with numbers in the corner to show how many pounds of ice were to be delivered. The iceman, armored in a rubberized apron, came in the heat of the summer's day, and we children waited on the parking between the street and the sidewalk, our bare feet hot in the brown grass but still cooler than on the searing paving.

The truck grumbled up and the iceman swung around to the back, threw up the tarp, and searched out a chunk of ice. We hoped there would be none of the right size so he'd have to take a pick and hack off a piece. He fixed his tongs, tried the weight on the spring scale at the back, and then strode off to the house. As soon as he was out of sight we scrambled after the chips of ice that might have fallen on the paving, and if he had not had to cut a big piece, we clambered up the back and reached after any chips that might have been lost among the sawdust. Some reckless ones among us might even take a stab at a big block with the pick. No confection ever tasted quite so good as the ice chips we sucked on those scorching days of our youth.

The extremes of fire and ice remain with me. There were the flameless fires of the peat bogs south of Clear Lake; though occasionally a tuft of grass would crackle alive, mostly there was a growing bed of ashes, heat, and a hazard to walking. The lake was very low in those years, and people feared it might disappear altogether. Clear Lake is a spring-fed shallow

125

dish, higher than the surrounding land, and a slight reduction in the flow from the springs brings forth reefs and rocks. The bogs along the south shore were dry, and they burned in sympathy with the heat of summer.

In later summers when I worked at the Boy Scout camp on the west end of the lake, I made the daily trip to Ventura for mail, odds and ends, and ice. How deliciously cool was the ice shed, the piles of soggy sawdust protecting the ice blocks cut last winter from the lake. I was never there to watch the harvest, the sawing and hauling during the dead of winter, but in the summer I could get a moment's reprise of the themes of winter songs. I wore shoes, usually, and the pavement was covered with dust, but the chips of ice still tasted good when my sense of dignity permitted me to pick one up.

Of course ice really belonged at the other end of the year. We lived on Willow Creek then, the outflow of Clear Lake to Lime Creek in Mason City and the "river" of Meredith Willson's River City. A few hundred yards downstream from our house were the bridge and park recreated by the musical. Somehow that small creek managed on occasion to flood even in the dry summers—a good rain would do it—but the spring floes of broken ice would jam together to dam up water. To protect upstream houses the authorities would dynamite the ice dams; crowds lined the shore to watch the big show. A man placed the charge, and then with a bang and a roar blocks of ice rose up, and water and ice rushed downstream over the permanent dams that had been built to power old mills, to provide water for lawns, or simply to make relatively ample pools to please the eye.

Just below the arched Music Man bridge one of those dams detoured water across the low area of East Park behind the band shell (where during the summer every Sunday and Wednesday nights the municipal band held forth; the old folks sat on the rows of green park benches or in parked cars; and adolescents roamed along the sides of the crowd, seeking out companions). In the spring flood the cakes spread out over the land near the shell. When the water went down, the cakes remained to rot in the sun and we boys ventured from our hill over the creek to go jumping from cake to cake. I suppose the main hazard was slipping into the ice-cold water about knee high, but it was for us the venture of exploration and the pleasure of what we were sure would have been forbidden had any adults known we were there.

This was not the delicious ice of summer, it was the dirty crumbling slushy ice that demonstrated an end to winter. Not that we had been pent up especially. Those were cold winters, and I recall that the school district had a rule that if at 8 A.M. the temperature was 15 below zero classes would be cancelled. We stared the lines off the thermometer each morning, because if it was cold enough, we'd be free to go outside. We wore leather boots calf high, brown corduroy knickers that whistled when we walked,

*"In later summers . . . I worked
at the Boy Scout camp
on the west end of the lake . . ."*

JIX (LEFT) AND A FRIEND, 1944.

leather coats with sheepskin linings, and stocking caps—a heavy load of wrapping—so while we moved, we were warm.

Winter ice had virtues. We skated on the frozen creek despite its real hazards. A few blocks upstream the water was used for cooling by the power company, and where it was put back into the creek were clouds of vapor that coated the trees and bushes with frost. By the time the water got to us it had cooled enough to freeze again, but during the doubtful seasons the ice was thin, tricky.

Once, while some boys were playing creek hockey with broken and taped sticks and a rock, a six-year-old strayed upstream toward the open areas and fell through. My brother rushed up the hill to our house for a ladder, which he slipped across the ice so he could crawl out to rescue the child. He had learned that from Boy Scouts. Fire trucks came eventually, and the paper showed his picture seated on the running board of the fire truck with the fireman, and later there were certificates and ceremonies. I was very proud, although I had missed the whole event, being uptown with my mother getting shoes. My brother was seven years older than I, so for me the events had no more reality than a story (like the one about how Dillinger robbed the local bank and the crowd of onlookers was so big the police had to hold their peace), but we didn't skate on the creek much after that.

Reality came more in shoveling snow off the sidewalks. The house we rented during the worst winters of the 30s had been built forty or fifty years earlier and later added to. It was grandly set back from the street on three acres of land and had a porch wrapping itself around the front and one side, a porte cocher with a landing block to enable folks to step from a carriage, a balcony, two-story white columns (Ionic), a bay window with curved glass, and a grand front hall with a grand front staircase. It also had steep backstairs, other stairs that led into a blank wall, a door that opened out over twelve feet of space, a solid wall where there might have been the best view of the woods and creek, the remnants of a formal rose garden, an interior pump room without a pump but with a dirt floor and another door that opened into space, a water heater in the kitchen you had to light when you wanted hot water, a coal furnace with a gas conversion unit, and a generally bleak rear end. My mother said the house had a Queen Anne front and a Mary Ann back. It certainly had long sidewalks that drifted deep in the winter. We'd all rally to help my brother shovel it; although I imagine that I was too small to be much help, the cold wind and the heavy crusted snow on which I could walk and the sense of duty to be done were real, as was the coal fire in the sitting room fireplace when we got inside.

I have survived other winters, but the ones between my eighth and twelfth years are the real ones. I have fleeting thoughts of ice skating on the city streets after an ice storm a few years later. Salting the streets was not then a killjoy game conducted to please an overscheduled society. I can also recall riding a balloon-tired bike two miles to ninth grade; the city streets were often snow rutted and I was the only one so consistently eccentric. As long as I could stand the cold I wore a cherry and silver satin athletic warm-up jacket; it was a thin but gaudy challenge to the dark jackets most people preferred. I can recall later a snowfall in September and winter camping in January, but after those first winters of outdoor adventuring, I found no others, really. Only a few moments since have rechilled the knee as through corduroy, refrosted the nose as through the wool stocking cap pulled down to the chin, or renipped the toes as when one's boots were laced too tight.

On the other hand the slush of spring always quickens my spirit. What fine dams we made against the curb! Lakes extended far into the street until some heedless driver created a tidal wave that wrecked the dam and sent cascades of water on down the street. I don't think we minded much because we simply had excuses then to build anew. Even yet in the spring I feel the urge to shovel channels through the slush, to make ponds—all in the name of clearing the gutter, of course. The sun sparkles on the water, the dirt on the snow is washed away, and nature offers a flourish of trumpets to wake the dead earth.

For me the chief function of spring was to get to summer. Oh, some people flew kites or (like Charlie Brown) didn't fly kites. There were May baskets with wild flowers instead of store candy; it was an excuse to go prowl the woods. Mosty there were violets, the yellow and dogtooth being prized, but bluebells and mayapples and Dutchman's britches and never-to-be-picked trillium were there too. And the spring brought Memorial Day; we climbed to the top of the highest building to raise the flag and admire the countryside, and we carried bunches of lilacs to strew from the high footbridge over Willow Creek in honor of the sailors. The storm windows came off, the screens went on, and we struggled through the last days of school. It was release.

Some summer days must have been cool and damp, but I recall only the hot broiling ones—or the ones with dramatic storms. We welcomed the gully washers because the storm sewers were much too small and certain streets were sure to flood. My mother knew them all, so we'd get in the car and seek them out, perhaps just driving through the curb-to-curb ponds (cars were built higher in those days, and a little caution would keep water out of the engine) and perhaps getting out to wade. Once when I was in high school, I was driving with suitable care through one of the flooded streets at midnight after a prom and I was smashed from the rear by someone who merely liked to see the water splash. I am now middle-aged cautious about driving in flooded streets, but I still share my mother's sense of irritation with spoilsports who make bigger sewers.

Magnificent storms rose over the lake. I missed the tornado (and despite all the horror pictures of recent years about the damage of tornadoes, for a long time I felt I had lost out on one of nature's dramas), but I recall winds that moved the water in the lake from the west end to the east; the boats and rafts were swept from our camp through the narrow channel between Lone Tree Point and the sandbar off MacIntosh Woods into the big east end of the lake. When the wind died, the water reversed itself and they came back of their own accord. One morning in such a storm a number of us went down to the lake to watch; when we returned huge trees had fallen across our path, tents were flattened and blown across the fields, and boys clinging to tent ropes were filled with adventure and bravado.

I cannot recall being hotter than when we had to lay pipe at the camp. When someone decided to extend water to individual campsites, it was understood that surface pipes were cheaper because unskilled labor was plentiful, so each year we put down and took up the sections of pipe that carried water to the distant washstands that were to encourage Scouts to be clean. While others performed the annual rituals of putting out and taking in the docks at the waterfront, I usually worked the pipes. In the grassy valley sheltered by heavy woods climbing the slopes, the sun bore down relentlessly, and the pipes had to be hauled by hand from the center of the camp. Swarms of mosquitoes skidded across my wet skin. Still, these modest nibbling furies contributed to the ultimate sense of victory when the water did indeed flow from the underground pump house to the farthest hill. They were part of the natural forces we had to learn to live with. Come evening, telling stories around the campfire, it was a matter of pride not to flinch, scratch, or slap while mosquitoes chewed on one's knees. I know the wisdom of my mother's remark that a dog has fleas so he won't spend too much time remembering that he is a dog. When we concentrated on mosquitoes we could forget we were boys.

There were idyllic moments too. Naming the stars in the constellations before the darkness was destroyed by city smog and lights. Resting on a branch high in a tree as a breeze rippled sunspots across the leaves. Greeting the dawn with meadowlarks. Images for a lifetime.

These are not the events of a great history; even local lore barely records such trivia, but lives are fashioned out of trivia. The storms were just bright red cherries on our chocolate sundaes. We survived the summer day by day. We waded the shallow waters of Willow Creek to catch guppy-sized minnows in our hands. Into bottles they went so that we could haul them up to dishpans kept behind the house. Every day we'd skim the surface of the ones that died during the night and then we'd seek more. I am not sure what we learned, and none of us became biologists or even fishermen, but it makes the imagery of childhood.

Recollections are selective. I remember some great events, but I don't feel that I am made from the stuff that schools teach as history. Snatches of the depression remain. I recall my mother's saying that my father was a sucker for anyone in need who wore a white beard like his father, and he noted that she had a weakness for any young boy like her sons. Dillinger robbed our bank and Mr. Shipley took a shot at Baby-Face Nelson from his office across the street, but I remember more clearly the limestone turret that graced his office building. Alf Landon whistle-stopped and Charles Lindbergh barnstormed, but whenever we went to Barrett Brothers grocery store I had to have an ice cream cone—"the cover charge," Mr. Barrett said. Great events and small were of the same order to me, although I can recall some of us grade schoolers puzzling out the astonishing size of the vote for Hitler in Austria, and by the time of Pearl Harbor we knew and didn't know what was important as our older friends went off to war and there were ration stamps and black marketeers and gold stars and reclaimed older teachers in the high school to replace the young ones who went to war. We collected paper and metal and did the odd jobs that ordinarily would have been reserved for men eighteen to twenty-six. And yet I recall these facts almost as one who has read a history book, as though the events were as remote as those relating to life in 1917–18, or even in 1861–65.

A decent psychologist/biographer would concentrate on people, some close, some symbolic. Mason City had writers and musicians. Martin and Tom Yoseloff, Hartzell Spence, Herbert Quick, Bil Baird, and Meredith and Dixie Stong Willson. Others like Phil Stong or Hamlin Garland seemed close. And bands and bandsmen were ever present—we expected to win firsts in all musical competitions. And the Rock Glen houses and the Park Inn hotel confirmed that my father's cousin Frank Lloyd Wright had connections with Mason City; and regular visits to Hillside, the school run by the Lloyd-Jones aunts where my mother and father met and where the Wrights trained architects, confirmed my sense that the arts were part of daily life. The library governed by Lydia Barrett had a superb collection for a small town and I used it indiscriminately to find books on the theories of sovereignty or economics for high school debates, the collected works of Bernard Shaw or Kipling or Conan Doyle, and whatever detective writers were current. Surely an apologist for the liberal arts should find his story among these ghosts.

Closer to me, though, are small ceremonies that gave structure to the day: candles at dinner, water to be heated for baths, Christmas trees to be lighted, dishes to be washed and wiped, and trash to be burned. Communion wafers and wine to be prepared, an Easter lamb cake to be cut, lawns to be mowed, cards to be played, and birthday cakes to be cut. New Year's goose to be carved, jigsaw puzzles to be assembled, Grandmother's dishes and Aunt Fannie's spoons to be set out, class plays to be acted, electric trains to be set up, and dogs to be fed. These indeed are not the great events that make histories but the repeated motions that make lives. And they are important.

That people were part of my world need not really be stated; they made the circumstances and were defined by them. With an older eye I know that they made me literally and figuratively, and yet I am not sure they belong in a child's view of the 30s and early 40s except as objects representing the place. At least, not for me. Do adults exist when you don't actually see them?

Of course, memory is the only existence the past has. We select and arrange the words to remake a past useful to us now. Images instead of ideas, or actions, or people come to me; I find only fire and ice. St. John would never have spit out that child's world, for in it there is no lukewarm. When everything exists for the first time, perhaps all is drama, and people, especially parents, are just the frame of the stage that stays always firm.

Tomorrow I might tell you a story with real people in it, their hearts bleeding and their eyes laughing. Or I might fashion a scholarly account of how developers of railroads created towns for the greater glory of commerce. I might on a colder day recall fondly the lives of those I love and recapitulate. But now scorched by the summer sun I must savor a bubble of air in a sliver of ice.

Robert Boston

ROBERT BOSTON'S essay, "Spring, 1955" (1976), focuses on a moment, unlike Winifred Van Etten's essay that follows and looks at a lifetime as a process of "growing up in Iowa." "I focus on this incident," says Boston, "because it was the one time in my life when I felt alienated from my own country. Traveling across the eastern part of the nation was like traveling through a country more alien than Germany was. But when I lay between the rows of that field, when I pressed myself to this earth, which had born and nurtured me, I was at home once again. I made my impression upon the earth, but the earth made an impression upon me as well, and I don't think I can ever become anything more or less than a child of this beautiful place, of this mundane place, of this vital place, this Iowa."

Robert Boston teaches writing at Iowa State University and with his wife lives on a farm near Boone. He was born at Webster City, Iowa, and both his parents came from farm families.

A Thorn for the Flesh (1973) is his first novel.

SPRING, 1955

TWENTY-ONE years ago. Seven of us creeping toward Iowa in a brand-new 1955 Dodge Coronet—V-8, stick shift, green-on-green two-tone. I had hoped for pink and black. Remember pink and black? Crazy, man! But my father had sent in the order from Germany so that the car would be waiting for us in New York. Maybe it was difficult to get the color you wanted by mail order. Or maybe he wanted green on green. Eleven years of wearing olive drab could accustom one to green, I suppose.

We had had to stay over in Frankfurt—measles epidemic, flu epidemic—I don't recall now, but it kept us there a week in quarantine, and I was glad. The Basler Hof was a hotel that felt like a movie set. A certain tidy decadence, or rather a feeling of age without decay, deep mattresses and ornate carpeting and woodwork lustrous with years of polishing, these were the Basler Hof, and while I should have been excited by the prospect of returning home after three years, I ached, I ached, at the thought of leaving Germany.

Somewhere on our journey from Ulm to Frankfurt I had bought a thick paperback book of American folk songs compiled by Alan Lomax, and I had been picking them through, strumming them on my guitar, during our stay in the Basler Hof. "Barbara Allen," "Foggy Foggy Dew," "Springfield Mountain." Playing them, I began to feel a kinship again with the States, an awareness that I had been gone too long.

But then one night, after I had gone to bed, after I had wrestled with wakefulness and had given up the effort to fall asleep, I got up and went to the wide casement windows to look into the night. The city illuminated the sky, but softly, so that if I looked upward I could see the velvet black of space and the pulsing points of the more brilliant stars. Looking down, I saw cobblestones glistening from rain or heavy dew—I don't remember which—glistening in the light of a single feeble street lamp, a scene that seemed almost unreal, for I had seen it so often in the movies: *The Third Man, The Desert Fox, The Man Between.* The heavy air muted far-off traffic, and below me, as if on cue, echoed the loneliest sounds I've ever heard.

One man, only one man walking the street in that great city, his footfalls the only clear sound in the muffling mist. I could not see him, for he was too directly below my window, walking, walking from where? To where? I don't know. Sometimes now I believe that he was going to or from nowhere, that he walked beneath that window only to complete the scene for me, to establish the mood and the direction of my thoughts. For as he walked, as he passed beneath my casement window, his leather heels knocking hollow on the cobblestones below, as he approached that solitary streetlight whose yellow gleams glistened on the dewy cobblestones, he began to whistle the most mournful, the most poignant song in the world.

I could not look for him to emerge into my field of vision. I was afraid that he was not there at all but was instead another vapor in the mist that shrouded the city, a vapor sent to remind me of the age and beauty and dignity of that conquered land that we now occupied.

I had climbed the spire of the cathedral in Ulm, a cathedral virtually completed when Columbus set sail westward. I had walked the worn corridors of medieval Heidenheim Castle, built on the bones of a Roman army outpost. I had seen the gap where Bonaparte had breached the wall of Ulm, and a few yards, a hundred and forty years, from that breach, a scarred concrete pillbox on the side of the hill. I had walked the streets of Ulm, streets eleven hundred years old. The rubble had long since been cleared from the streets, had been dumped back into the cellars of the bombed-out buildings, half of the buildings in the city. I had heard the polka bands playing in the festooned barges on the Danube in the spring, had heard the laughter and the music of the carnivals. I had heard, too, the shriek of the trains in the night, a shriek more agonized than any Casey Jones could have heard. And I had walked the hills and forests near the town, the hilly pastures clipped by sheep, the forests ordered row on row; and from those hillsides miles from town, I'd seen the lofty spire rise, a hundred and sixty-one meters high. And I had walked among the people in drab wet winter as they plodded the streets. I had played among them in the summer, sporting with them in the icy mountain water of the Iller, a romping stream that raced by Ulm.

And that whistler, that solitary walker in the glistening black street below my window, brought these things to mind as he approached the lamplight, whistling "Lili Marlene."

Now we crawled westward in that green-and-green Dodge, white sun broiling the New Jersey Turnpike, the Pennsylvania Turnpike. The country was greening, the hills and fields alive, and I should have been happy to be home again. But I hated it. I yearned for the cool spring, for the subdued atmosphere of Germany.

Our MATS airliner, a rattling DC-7, had landed at midnight in Springfield, Massachusetts. Fatigue dulled my senses. Fourteen hours in the air, a seat on the wing where the roar of the engines and the nagging shocks of turbulent air had driven sleep away. A stubble-faced cab driver

*"Eleven years of wearing olive drab
could accustom one to green . . ."*

BOSTON'S FATHER AND GRANDFATHER BEFORE GOING TO GERMANY.

chewed a cigar and spat out the window as he drove us to the Springfield train station. "Yeah, them Red Sox ain't worth a damn this year. None o' them teams is worth a damn. Let them niggers play, and the game just goes to hell. Know what I mean?"

Two-by-four hamburger joint across the street from the station. Smoke and rancid grease. My sister and I were sent to buy food for all of us while our parents waited in the station, trying to placate the hungry young children, eighteen months to five years old. The guy behind the counter was from some cartoon—greasy T-shirt, sagging belly. "Hell no, I ain't got no sack to carry it in. You tell 'em they wanna eat they gotta c'mere." I explained about the children, and he began to rummage among the debris below the counter, cursing. Finally came up with a flyspecked paper bag, dumped the burgers into it, and squashed it on the counter. "Ketchup? You wanted ketchup you shoulda said something, kid. You ordered ten burgers. That's what you got. Now get 'em outta here. Or you want me to carry 'em for you too?" A cop seated at the counter laughed, and we stumbled out the door.

The train to New York was a garish affair of chrome and tattered red plastic. A commuter train, evidently, for it stopped every few miles. Soon all the seats were filled, and people began to pile up in the aisles. My father and I sprawled in our seats, dozing in spite of the glaring lights and the heat and smell of close-packed bodies. "You'd think some *gentleman* would offer a lady his seat." Whining voice above me. I pretended to sleep. "Guess they ain't gentlemen," said another voice. "You can say that again." Something, a purse, probably, banged against my head. I ignored it.

A cafeteria in Grand Central Station. We sat beside the serving line, finishing our ham and eggs and toast. A slender Negro man stood in the line, dressed in a delicate dove grey suit and patent leather shoes. A bit of lace showed at his wrist as he pointed at something in the steam table. "Oh, my, that looks absolutely luscious! I must have some, but it will simply destroy my waistline."

"Jesus Christ!" My father swallowed hard and stood up. "Let's get out of here." And I thought, yes, let's go to Idlewild and get on the first plane to Frankfurt. To home.

Instead, we vegetated in the Saint George Hotel. Threadbare carpets. Steam-sodden food, tasteless paste. Old people ranged in rows in the lobby watching a flickering Sylvania TV. Ed Sullivan's "Toast of the Town." Georgia Gibbs singing "Dance with Me, Henry." Vapid, neutered version of "Work with Me, Annie," by Hank Ballard and the Midnighters, which we had heard in Germany for months. And in the basement, sharp-faced kids in T-shirts and leather jackets played at pinball and sharpshooter machines. One day, our second day there, some of them stole a purse from a woman in the lobby. Mom made us stay in the room after that.

"Grandma's kitchen. . . . Grandpa's Copenhagen and the rifle by the door."

THE HOUSE NORTH OF WEBSTER CITY

Then, the green-on-green Dodge pulled up in front and some kid not much older than me drove us to where we couldn't miss the Jersey Turnpike. He said nothing, obviously contemptuous because we couldn't find our way out of town. I don't know how he got back to the car dealership. I hope he didn't make it.

We headed westward. New Jersey, Pennsylvania, Ohio, Indiana rolled by in the night. Georgia Gibbs begged Henry to dance with her at least twice an hour. The new-car smell gave way to the odors of sweat and cigarettes, vomit and dirty diapers. The children cried and squabbled through the night. And then the dawn and squalid South Chicago. We rolled through it in silence, a city more tragic, more completely destroyed, than Ulm with its blocks and blocks of bombed-out buildings. The people more hopeless, more defeated, than the old women I had seen near the Bahnhof at Dachau, black-shawled women picking bits of coal from the railroad right-of-way. Here no picturesque cobblestone streets glistening in the evening dew but raw concrete steaming in the morning sunlight. Here no plaintive, whistled "Lili Marlene" but the coarse, raucous sounds of Joe Turner and Clyde McPhatter and their rhythm-and-blues tunes.

After that, the land looked better, more familiar. New shoots of corn and beans, new blades of tender oats, and I could feel belonging coming, coming, growing with each mile. The memories came inching back as that green Dodge inched westward. The memories of summer nights and lightning bugs aswirl on nearby fields and lawns. Lightning bugs. I could not remember seeing them in Europe. This to see again. And real woods, not just garden plots of trees so neatly pruned and rowed with underbrush all weeded out. The hanging vines of Grandpa's grove, the tangled shrubs that made hide-and-seek a challenge. And the muddy-banked Boone River, where we'd sat and teased the bullheads and the catfish or whatever else would come to clamp their jaws about our hooks.

Not the rock-imprisoned Danube or the frothing little Iller, but a stream where willows shaded you, where bobbers floated lazy in the summer afternoons, where ancient turtles sunned themselves on fallen logs, disorderly but natural. Who would bother, who would dare, to brick up a bed for the lazy Boone, to haul a soggy log away from where it had fallen, belonging there? Belonging there. I felt belonging coming as I watched the land grow richer, blacker, bigger as it rolled beneath us.

Then, the Mississippi at Dubuque, stretching wide from Illinois to Iowa, flowing dark, majestic, diminishing the Danube in my mind. And after Dubuque came the other names, the roadside names, the names I had forgotten or had buried in my memory. They all came marching back on signs that pointed straight ahead or north or south. I did not need to see the towns; their names were enough, even though the towns themselves lay forty-two miles off our route. Every road sign flashing past struck sparks of recognition. Every road sign lit my way back home.

Dyersville, Manchester, Independence, straight ahead. To the north of us lay Oelwein (horrid name, if you know German), and south was Cedar Rapids. Then Waterloo and Cedar Falls. The land was growing all around us, green and green, as the Dodge rolled onward, green-on-green, toward the west, toward the magic names whose spells increased their holds upon my memories. Parkersburg and Ackley ambled by, then Iowa Falls, where Bob and Mary lived, and Alden, "The Best Town by a Dam Site," where Grandpa'd umpired baseball once. And then the names of home appeared: Williams, Blairsburg, Webster City.

Stop. The giddy aftermath of motion. Wobbly legs. The sudden rush of silence after hours of engine roar and wind noise. The children shy, hiding behind Mom's skirt, avoiding Grandma's smothering hugs and Grandpa's bristly kisses. Grandma's kitchen. Bitter coffee cut with cream and sugar. Grandpa's Copenhagen and the rifle by the door. Sounds of hogs and cattle. The faint odor of manure. And the fields. The fields reaching away to forever, black and warm. Rows of corn and beans, golden green, pushing upward, stretching toward the sun.

I, the son come home. Fifteen years old, and I felt wiser than a patriarch, for I had a knowledge in me. Some knowledge of the world, it's true, but that was not important. Seeing Germany, being there and loving it, did not make me German. And I knew that my eyes would never have the ferretlike sharpness and wile I'd seen in the eyes of those young New York hoods. My knowledge was not theirs.

After supper, I went into the cornfield south of the barnyard. It was just sunset, and the western sky glowed gold. I lay face down between the rows and stretched my arms full length toward the sun. The earth was warm and soft beneath me, and I breathed deep, smelling, smelling, smelling the heavy smell of earth, tasting earth on my tongue. The new corn rustled slightly in the breeze, and I lay there for a long time. The knowledge surged within me. I dug my fingers deep into the black earth, gripping tightly, pulling myself downward against it. I was of this earth, this earth and no other. Like the corn, I drew my sustenance from it. I belonged to it, and it to me. I felt warm, secure, an infant in my mother's lap.

When I finally stood, the stars were coming out, still feeble in the twilight. And, as I looked down, I could see my imprint in the earth.

"I, the son come home."

BOSTON, AGE 17, AND HIS DOG PEDRO.

Winifred M. Van Etten

WINIFRED VAN ETTEN was born and reared in Emmetsburg; since the mid-1930s and her marriage to Bernard Van Etten, she has lived at Mount Vernon. In her undergraduate years at Cornell College, she came under the influence of Professor Clyde "Toppy" Tull and his wife, Jewell, two marvelous teachers of literature and writing. At first she wrote short stories for the *Husk,* the Cornell literary magazine. Then in 1936 her only novel, *I Am the Fox,* won the $10,000 novel prize offered by the Atlantic Monthly Press and Little, Brown and Company "for the most interesting and distinctive contribution" to their annual contest.

In the years since, Winifred Van Etten, who holds the M.A. from Columbia, has taught English literature and composition courses at Cornell from which she is now retired. She has done very little public writing in the years since her novel other than a portion of a centennial pageant for Cornell in 1953.

As "Three Worlds" reveals, she has not lost the sure touch that once produced an outstanding novel. Mrs. Van Etten treats all her life as "a growing up in Iowa" period, so her contribution to this book varies considerably from the others. That is why I have placed it last.

THREE WORLDS

SOMEPLACE in the family archives there is a large mounted photograph. It shows my father standing in the midst of his field of corn. He was a tall man, six feet two or more, and he was stretching as far as he could above his head to hang his derby hat on the highest ear of corn he could reach. There were higher ears, but this one was the best he could do. We lived on the edge of town and just beyond the town limits he had seven acres of land that he treated as a garden. No weed dared intrude. In the days when forty or forty-five bushels an acre was usual he in some years produced one hundred. As a child I assumed that a hundred bushels was normal. Sometimes I was allowed to help with the plowing. I drove the team; my father walked behind guiding the plow. When I reached the point at which, coming to the end of a row, I could turn the team, reverse the direction, and start back the other way without tearing up any corn hills, I regarded myself as an expert.

These were the days of the tall corn in Ioway.

Years later my husband and I picked up a hitchhiker from Connecticut. We noticed him staring at the crops along the highway. Finally, he spoke. "I don't think it's so very tall," he said. Obviously the only thing he had ever heard about Ioway (at least he did not confuse it with Ohio or Idaho) was that it is the place where the tall corn grows.

We tried to explain to him that tallness was no longer an object. No more did farmers cut their tallest stalks and take them to town where rival mast-high specimens stood in a row in front of the bank. The corn picker had put an end to the tall corn. Uniformity was now the goal, and Ioway was the place where the tall corn grew—once—but now conformed to the demands of machines. Uniformity—that was the criterion of excellence. In Iowa. Ioway was gone.

THE FIRST WORLD / *The Prairie*

Ioway was my first world, the world of my very early childhood. No buffalo roamed there, but it was still pretty close to true prairie. We took long excursions across it. Rover trotted along in front, tail waving as debonairly as though he had not already covered many miles. Trinket stepped it off lightly, five people and a surrey apparently nothing to her flying slender legs. We had been on the way since before dawn on our annual trip to visit an uncle who lived fifty miles north of us near the Minnesota border. We had shivered at first in the morning chill, but now it was getting warm and there were many miles still to go. Fifty miles in a day for one horse pulling a carriage and five people was a long journey, but the trip could be made no other way. There was no railroad, hardly anything that could even be called a road, only a sometimes barely discernible trace through the tall prairie grass, and as we got farther north, skirting the edges of a big slough, there was water standing along or on what passed for a road. Now and then a fox eyed us suspiciously, and once an animal my father said was a wolf sent delicious chills through us as we recalled those stories of Russians tossing first one passenger then another from their vehicle to delay the ravening wolves.

But this wolf, if it was a wolf, seemed of a mind to tend to its own business or else it was of a peaceful disposition. Everything was peace: a soft June morning, banks of wild roses, the tall grasses, the reeds and cattails. The bobwhites whistled, the meadowlarks sang. Even my father sang. He couldn't carry a tune, but there were two lines of one ditty that he droned over and over in his monotone as we rode along. I never heard him sing more than the two lines and never except on the occasion of one of these family safaris:

> Oh, green was the grass on the road, on the way
> And bright was the dew on the blossoms of May.

Sometimes we all sang, mostly hymns, since those were the songs we all knew. We did the Crusaders' Hymn over and over. It seemed to fit this lovely, lonely world through which we were passing.

> Fair is the meadow
> Fairer still the woodlands
> Robed in the blooming garb of spring.
> Jesus is fairer, Jesus is purer
> Who makes the woeful heart to sing.

I was never a religious child in any conventional way, but somehow I sensed a connection between the woodlands, the meadow, and that purity we were taught to call Jesus at Sunday school. The son of God and man was a concept beyond me, the Holy Ghost complete befuddlement, but fairest Lord Jesus, the fair meadow, the fair woodlands, these gave me an intuition of oneness that, without owning the capacity to think about it, I felt included me.

"Everything was peace: a soft June morning, banks of wild roses, the tall grasses, the reeds and cattails."

STILL EXISTING VIRGIN PRAIRIE ON A RAILROAD RIGHT-OF-WAY NEAR MONONA.

Dark would be falling by the time we reached my uncle's farm, all of us hungry, all so dead tired that even the mattresses stuffed with corn husks felt and smelt good and whispered and rustled soothingly. In the morning there would be prayers in the neat little living room with its center table bearing a ten-pound Bible with Doré illustrations, a tall kerosene lamp, its double globes hand painted with flowers, perhaps a big rosy shell on the lower shelf. Of course there was the cottage organ. If the decor was what every housewife felt it should be, there would be on the organ shelves some small ornaments; a china boot; a fancy box or two; and crowning glory of home decorations, a tall vase of peacock feathers. Such proofs of culture could only be surpassed by a stereopticon set by means of which we acquainted ourselves with far climes and countries while gaudy Japanese wind chimes tinkled in the open window. It never occurred to us that we might actually sometime see these places ourselves.

Our world was bounded by what amounted to a slightly modified frontier to the north of us and to the south the little town from which we had come. The town, a sort of rough excrescence on the smoothness of the prairie, had mud streets and electric light only in the stores except for a few affluent residences and those who had their own Delco systems. But it had the county courthouse and the jail, and once in a while an automobile was to be seen, usually driven by some young blade viewed with as much disapproval as one of Hell's Angels would be a half century later. Such a monster, if my mother was driving, would set Trinket prancing on her hind legs until some gallant from the sidewalk came out and held her head until the horror had passed.

The town had eight churches: six Protestant, two Catholic, plus a Catholic grade school and the quarters for the nuns and priests. God's Geese (the nuns), so-called by one of our family friends always admired for the rightness of her views, were seldom seen on the streets, but we were conscious of their presence just as we were of some sinister existence in the priest's house. The town also had at one time according to my elders nine saloons. One story said that an Irish emigrant came out in the early days, set a jug of whiskey down on the prairie, and the town grew up around it and fell at once to fighting as though Cadmus had sown the dragon's teeth there and not in Greece. For it was a divided town, half Irish Catholic, half Protestant, a mixture of Scandinavians, Germans, Scots, and English, the latter two often referred to as "remittance men" because their money was remitted to them from the old country.

But for my family the most important element in the town was the existence of three weekly papers, two Catholic and Democrat (they were considered one and the same thing), one Protestant and Republican of which my father was the owner and editor. No issue was too small for a Battle of the Boyne and my father was always in the midst of the fray. He used to try to prevent our seeing the other two papers, but somehow we always found out what he was being accused of that week. Sometimes he was said to have been found lying drunk in the gutter (he who was a teetotaler) surrounded by dead soldiers. At other times, in fact at all times, he was up to some political skulduggery designed to keep Catholics and Democrats out of their rights. Nearly every week there was recorded some new villainy on his part, and my view of my native town was colored for years by these bitter battles. For bitter they were. What goes on in Ulster today seems more comprehensible to me because of the tenacious feuding imported to this peaceful prairie from the Old World. Even the dogs were Catholic or Protestant. On a Saturday my brother would take Rover, cross the tracks to the south side, and there take on all comers, whether curs or Catholics, in epic battle. Few of us, however, were really personal enemies.

One of my most abhorred duties as a young girl was "to meet the trains." There were trains in those days, two of them, the Milwaukee and the Rock Island, two each way, each day. When everyone else in the office was too busy, I had to do this chore. "Meeting the train" meant walking to the depot, going up to each person who bought a ticket and inquiring who he was, where he was going, and why. An ally and helper, a great icebreaker, was Rover's successor, Old Shep. He was a stray that had learned to be a station beggar until he adopted us. But he still met the trains, spotted everyone who appeared to be carrying a lunch and, though a big dog, sat up on his hind legs before his victims and tried to look underfed. He usually got something and so did I—many a handout I would not otherwise have had the courage to ask for.

Another ally, truly unexpected, was the train meeter of the rival paper, a middle-aged man, who out of pure pity for my shyness often handed over gratis some of his own garnerings. After that I was never able really to believe that all Democrats and Catholics, one and the same thing of course, were children of mischief. Still, any exception to the rule was rare and change came to Ioway very slowly. After I had become a schoolteacher, I overheard at a club meeting one middle-aged woman whisper to another behind her hand in the tone of one relating a shocking scandal about another person present, "You know, she's a Democrat."

On the other hand, one of my Ulsterite father's best friends was a priest, who for years on their wedding anniversary, sent my parents a gift of silver, a spoon, a cold meat fork, a ladle. I do not remember him, but his name was that of a friend in our house for years.

Later I came to see that probably my father hadn't minded as much as the rest of the family did. For he was Irish too, an Orangeman, and though he wanted to be sure he was on the right, the moral, side of a controversy, the fact remained that he loved a fight for its own sake. It was not so nice for his daughters. In spite of an occasional detente there were many times when we hated to go out in public or to be seen on the streets. We yearned for the day when we could go to college and become teachers, somewhere, anywhere except at home. It never occurred to us or to anyone else that we could do anything except teach. What else could a nice girl do? She filled in the time between high school or college and marriage by teaching—for pin money, for funds for filling a hope chest, or simply for something to do. One difference for us was no hope chests. In our family it was not expected that we would marry, for only one man in the world was fit to marry, our mother had married him, and it followed logically that we would do nothing so morally equivocal as to marry at all. The teaching itself with a few notable exceptions was not really very important to anyone, the students, the teacher herself, the community. About all that was required of her was "to keep order in the classroom."

I remember vividly some of the women who toured the state campaigning for women's suffrage. Strange creatures, they seemed to me. Normally a woman's public appearances were confined to reading in mincing, ladylike tones a "paper" to her social club. But these women stood up and talked straight out as though they didn't even realize they were women. Since my parents were strong believers in votes for women, one or two of these campaigners were our house guests, and we heard many anecdotes of their adventures that we would not have heard in a public meeting. They laughed about them, but they were bruised; the obscene remarks made to them on the streets; the filthy places in which they sometimes had to stay, collapsing country hotels patronized chiefly by bedbugs, hamlets with no hotel at all where they stayed in some private home and got revolting food to eat. One told of having to swallow for breakfast eggs boiled (it was washday) in the same boiler in which the family's clothes were simmering; the stern disapproval of most of the men and the timid reluctance of most of the women to say what they really felt. How proud I was when my mother stood up at a meeting in the county courthouse and spoke for five minutes on the issue. Of course, she was a university graduate and had been a teacher. What could you expect from such ruined females?

The day my mother went to the polls and cast her first ballot was a prideful occasion. She voted, no protest, exactly as my father "suggested" to her. And when I cast my first vote as a college senior, my father saw to it that I received an absentee ballot and a list of "suggestions" about various candidates. It never occurred to me or my father that there was anything out of the way about this manner of exercising one's citizenship. After all, what did I know about politics? I had been taking courses in history and government, but all that was theory. The thing was to know the candidates. This sort of thing occurred long after my fundamental attitudes had been fixed in childhood.

For us, young females, the world was a place governed by taboos. The stern Calvinist morality we inherited from one side amalgamated with a late Victorian gentility in a way that produced some pretty potent forbiddings. The taboo was usually related to sex, of course. Anything a girl did that in any way resembled what a boy or man did was taboo. Looking back, I can understand some of these forbiddings; others seem totally incomprehensible.

Taboo: A girl must not part her hair on the side. Boys wore theirs that way.

Taboo: Everybody knew about the bad end to which whistling girls came. In some quarters, it was no joke.

Taboo: Legs didn't even get mentioned. Before leaving for church on a Sunday morning, each of us was stood up in front of the east door through which the summer sun sent stabbings of light. If there was the slightest sign of a shadow, back we went to put on another petticoat. I have worn as many as five. I used to entertain myself in church by imagining all those buttons simultaneously bursting off and all those petticoats descending in starched white heaps to the floor. They were fun to iron, too, with "sadirons" (no object was ever more accurately named) heated on a coal-burning range. Shirts for three men. Petticoats for four women—each petticoat with a flounce, each flounce with a ruffle, each ruffle with embroidered or lace trimming consisting of two or three rows of "insertion" and a final lace frill.

Summer or winter females wore hats in the house of God; St. Paul said they had to. My hair was tied with a ribbon at the top of my head. The stiff crown of the hat pressed hard on the ribbon knot, held by an elastic under the chin, well chewed in an effort to loosen it a little. The result was that I spent nearly every Sunday afternoon lying in the hammock nauseated with headache and making occasional dashes for the porch railing.

Taboo: Card playing. Whenever cards were mentioned my mother saw the Devil, horns, hooves, and tail complete.

Taboo: Dancing. There were whispered tales of dissolute girls who checked their corsets in the cloakrooms at the public dance halls in order to "enjoy as much sensual pleasure from the dancing as possible."

Taboo: Looking into the open doors of a blacksmith shop as you went by.

Taboo: Walking on any street where there was a saloon.

Taboo: Walking by the horse doctor's office or the livery stable.

Taboo: Scraping your feet on the sidewalk. I got mud on my shoes one day, and when I tried to scrape it off on the sidewalk the elders with me fairly snarled reproof.

Taboo: Walking close to a business place in basement quarters. You were to take to the outer edge of the sidewalk lest some lascivious male might look up and be filled with glee to discover that you had legs.

Taboo: Owning a dog. No nice girl had a dog of her own. The family dog was all right, but as a piece of personal property the dog was taboo, especially if it was a female. The owner might as well advertise her profession.

The sheer irrationality of most of these notions not surprisingly led before too many years had passed to the so-called revolt of youth.

Actually, there was little for any young person to do, even those not reared in so austere a regime as ours. There was a lake, weedy, muddy, and scummy, but it had several small islands, one, our favorite, about the size of a haystack, good for picnicking. Later the lower end of the lake was dredged and became a favorite playground for many. Naturally no fastidious person would go into the water. After all, who knew what was going on down there under the surface? It couldn't be for nothing that those prickly wool swimsuits sold in the stores carried the label, "Urine rots wool." We could go in far up the lake, the undredged part, where some of our farming friends had houses close to shore. But the first time I tried it I came out covered with leeches. I nearly screamed myself into spasms while my country friend matter-of-factly plucked them off one by one, leaving me streaming a pale mixture of blood and water. Eventually the town made a park, its trees still baby-sized, and put in a tennis court and some swings. The park was little used for a while. Tennis, like that other foreign game, golf, or pasture pool as we called it, was for effete foreigners like the remittance men. We had the true bumpkin mentality. Whatever was outside our limited experience was bound to be either wicked or ludicrous.

The high school had a football team, but athletics were certainly not overemphasized in the schools. I never saw a gymnasium until I went to college. Once in a while we were made to stand between the rows of classroom desks and wave our arms and bend our knees and feel silly. This was called calisthenics and happened only occasionally. What we did get was a core of required courses and a very few electives: four years of English, four of history or civics, four of mathematics, and a language, Latin or German (until the First World War when French patriotically replaced German). I had a remarkable Latin teacher as a result of whose influence I studied Latin for four years and went on to another four in college. I had another reason to be grateful to her. Girls were required to take domestic science (no one called it home economics) in the seventh, eighth, and ninth grades. I loathed it so much that in the seventh and eighth grades I never would have passed if my teacher, who roomed next door to us, had not taken pity on me and finished my aprons and nighties herself. Now as I entered high school I swallowed my fear of the formidable Latin teacher–principal and begged off the domestic science requirement. There was sympathy in her soul someplace, for she let me take courses in physiology and "physical geography" instead. Perhaps she, like me, was a feminist in the cradle. It did not take me long to observe that taboos applied to girls more frequently and more firmly than to boys.

The son was able to escape. His sisters could not. We were in effect in-carcerated. Therefore I hated being a girl.

Before I had ever seen or heard of a penis I envied boys. Freud, I knew when I read him years later, was wrong altogether about the envy of the female for the male. I envied males because their very existence con-ditioned and controlled mine. Femaleness was a condition of innate in-feriority. When I once confided to our family doctor that I, too, would like to become a doctor when I grew up, he laughed his booming laugh. "Ha, ha. A hen Medic!" Clearly, an obviously absurd idea. I gave it up on the spot.

What it came down to was this. A female was both inferior and for some unknown reason obscene. The best thing a girl could do was to pretend she didn't exist. Her best strategy was silence and a poker face.

Even girls reared in a more lenient pattern than ours had no greater freedom of choice. Teach. Be a stenographer. Be a nurse. Even nursing was suspect. I heard a mother telling her daughter just what kind of duties she as a nurse would be expected to perform for male patients. "And nine times out of ten the man for whom she does these things will insult her." A sexual insult then was something only slightly less appalling than rape is now.

My first theatrical experience was a heady trip to the local nickelodeon. What was offered there (fare five cents) was ordinarily deemed trash but this time *The Odyssey* and *The Last Days of Pompeii* were to be shown. These two were considered educational. They proved at least unforgettable; the smoke belching from the upside down ice cream cone of Vesuvius, Scylla thrusting out head one and snatching a Greek, then head two and nabbing another, then at precise mechanical intervals head three and the rest. I saw her in dreams for years.

Thirty years later when audiovisual aids were the modish thing in educational circles, my English department, feeling the obligation to be up-to-date, ordered a catalogue, examined it, found there a film of *The Odyssey* (which our classes were at the time reading), sent for the film, showed it. Lo, it was the precise film I had seen as a child at the nickelodeon. I collapsed in mirth and so did all the students. Onward and upward with the arts. The majesty of *The Odyssey* must have stayed with that group forever.

But there were better things in that town.

The town did have aspirations to culture. The women's clubs worked hard and intelligently on worthwhile studies and projects. The men had a weekly debating club characterized by furious differences of opinion. There was an adequate opera house. Maude Adams played there. Schumann-Heink sang. We heard, oh wonder, a major symphony or-chestra. There was a lyceum course and, inevitably in a self-respecting town, a chautauqua where we swallowed huge gobbets of culture and were rewarded at the end with a play (always a farce or a melodrama) or a "humorous lecturer." It was William Jennings Bryan and "A Cross of Gold" to Strickland Gilliland and "Bibbety, Bob."

The town had two or three highly trained musicians. They shook their heads over the introduction of the phonograph, "canned," machine-made music. They were seers. The opera house soon became a motion picture theater, and no more road companies visited the town. Mothers need worry no longer about their sons hanging around stage doors. Instead they could wonder what they were up to in those Tin Lizzies.

What does growing up mean? I thought at one time that it meant that one had arrived at an immutable view of life and the world. The grown-ups I knew never seemed to change. They had all the answers, the same yesterday, today, and forever. But such a definition of growing up did not apply to a child of the twentieth century. I grew up all over again in each of my three worlds.

That first world of my early childhood was bucolic, idyllic, and, I believed at the time, everlasting. We knew, naturally, that there had been wars and torturers in the past. But those things were relics of ancient evil. They could never happen again. It was still to us, just emerging from childhood, a world of peace.

THE SECOND WORLD / Gopher Prairie

That child's world abruptly ended with the outbreak of World War I. It almost destroyed those innocent, provincial conceptions of my childhood. But not quite. We still had our faith in our American right-ness. Even if the President was a Democrat, we were making the world safe for democracy. Our kind of world would prevail. We were putting a stop forever to that evil anachronism, war.

The war had its compensations, too. Though remote, it was exciting, a kind of melodrama itself with a satanic villain to hate, and dozens of nice songs, sweet or jolly, and grown-up girls marrying soldiers and weeping on the railroad platform as they left.

I remember the end of the war. In the middle of the night a truck manned by loud-voiced citizens with megaphones toured the streets shouting, "Germany has signed the armistice terms. Germany has signed the armistice terms." My father put his head out the window and roared. Then he sped to town to join the dancing, shouting celebration in the streets. We stayed at home. Girls, you know. I still relive my white rage as I lay that night in bed and listened to the revelry afar. Bed in my opinion was no place to spend a night like this one. The next night there was a proper, organized celebration with many speeches and all moral things of that kind. To that we went. And learned again that justice, goodness, and Americanism had triumphed. Our faith had been vindicated. Before too long, however, there would begin an erosion of that faith. Some not too much older than we were already thinking of the world as a place where war was inevitable, and each new war sadder and uglier than the last.

I was, in years, no child by now. Though still in high school, I was aware of fierce controversies and undercurrents of feuds on an international scale that seemed a sad magnification of the feuds and little wars of my home town. Inside ourselves, little had changed. Therefore war. But external changes came furiously. We found them delightful. The car was the great emancipator of youth. Those brothels on wheels drove our elders crazy though they were as mad about them as their offspring who, if they considered themselves of the intelligentsia, left the Prairie behind with all possible speed to live in Greenwich Village. Paris would have been better but next best was the Village where Ioway origins, Iowa itself, could be forgotten or concealed, and the frenzied world of Fitzgerald was the model, with his "gold-hatted, high bouncing lovers."

But those of us who attended small, midwestern colleges scarcely knew we were living in the Jazz Age. Nor did we know that we belonged to the Lost Generation.

Of the writers of the period, Sinclair Lewis gave us the hardest jolt. There wasn't much resemblance between the way he presented Gopher Prairie and the Prairie we thought we knew. That anyone should describe it as a place where "dullness was deified, dullness was God" was at first unthinkable. But the thinking ones thought and many ended by repudiating their childhood, the American past, and America itself. They had grown to a new stage. They were in revolt against war, against the "back to normalcy" of Harding, proud product of the Middle West. Even those of us who stayed in the Middle West didn't want to go back. We didn't want normalcy, which we now interpreted as Babbittry, and viewed the ordinary American as "Boobus Americanus." For Mencken was our guru. He revealed normalcy to us as an abomination. We went about carrying copies of the *American Mercury* to prove how sophisticated we were though far from Paris where all the sad young men held forth, and Hemingway's Parisian expatriates and roving alcoholics were in reality as alien to us as Fitzgerald's frenetic youth. Actually, Fitzgerald was not as alien as we thought him to be if we had read him right. He blinded us by his glitter. We did not discern that he was writing of the death of the American Dream, that prairie land of innocence from which he too had originally come.

But Boobus Americanus we knew. He lived next door. He was Babbitt, Elmer Gantry, the Rotarian, the booster, the flapper, the campus sheik with his coonskin coat and unbuckled galoshes. Above all, he was a Methodist as were most of us. To Mencken there was something very very funny about a Methodist. It was startling to learn that we were boobs. Perhaps we were so ready to accept Mencken because we already were feeling that this was not necessarily the best of all possible worlds. In 1931 the tomb of the Unknown Soldier was completed and inscribed.

> Here rests in
> Honored glory
> An American Soldier
> Known but to God.

But the glory and the honor had somehow faded. The war had then been fought for nothing. Prohibition increased lawlessness, the presence of women at the polls failed to produce the purification of politics expected of it. The government was corrupt. You could take your choice: since the dream was gone, you might as well have fun—bounce, bounce, bounce. Or settle down, make a living, make if possible more than a living, get rich. Be a Babbitt.

But that didn't work out either. Our elders had been telling us all along: "Come boom, come bust." And "bust" came. The period between the wars was almost two different eras, boom and bust queerly combined.

In midwestern colleges there had never been much boom. Nor had the mores changed much. Maybe the boys found a jazz age off campus someplace. On campus girls still had to be in at eight o'clock. The doors were locked. One minute's tardiness drew penalties. When it was discovered that fire escapes could provide exit from or to things other than fires, the screens on the escapes were nailed shut. "Better to burn here than hereafter," quipped one faculty member in a committee set up to survey safety conditions on campus.

Many students lived in conditions of incredible poverty. When the banks closed, we thought the end of the world had come. And we could see another war in the making. Instead of an anachronism war was turning into a chronic condition. Four freedoms tried hard to take the place of making the world safe for democracy, but it was a sad war hated even by those who conceded it had to be fought. And if war were a chronic disease, it must be that it proceeded from something in ourselves. Like the creeping horrors I now knew existed under the fair meadow where a praying mantis could teach men lessons in ingenious cruelty, it must be that there was some horror in ourselves. Boobus Americanus was admirable compared to what we now saw ourselves to be.

The night World War II came to an end I happened to be spending in a berth in a sleeping car. I did not sleep. At every station stop, I raised the blind a few inches and peeked out at the sorry little knots of trying-to-celebrate citizens. Before I left home there had been an impromptu gathering to take note of the end of war. It couldn't be called a celebration. It was more like a prayer meeting. I did not go. I felt it just as well not to call God's attention to what we had been up to on this planet if by some good fortune his attention had been fixed on some other part of the universe at the time. The bomb put an end forever to any good I had hoped might come from the war. Not for one moment did I believe those who were saying that this was the ultimate weapon, so hideous that war could never be used again lest we prove T. S. Eliot wrong and end the world with a bang, not a whimper. Sooner or later the bomb would be used. Whenever had men invented some fascinating, lethal toy and refrained from using it? I said a word I wouldn't even have heard in my childhood. The bomb would be used just because we had it.

This was my last growing up. I no longer expected any sort of change that involved a change in persons. I couldn't foresee all the uses of nuclear energy in addition to the bomb. All I saw was Hiroshima.

Now it was not Lewis, not Fitzgerald, not Mencken who came to mind. It was Hemingway. I had thought I hated him for seeing what he thought he saw in bullfights. Now I believed he was right. A bullfight was simply something in us coming out.

He was right, too, about our loneliness. We were not merely a lost generation but a lost humanity. A few "clean, well-lighted places" were to be found where chronic loneliness became more bearable. But loneliness was palpable. Every celebrator on the station platforms looked lonely. In every crowd each looked separate, alone.

I recalled the celebrating at the end of the first war. Then we were "we" or had thought so. But this time was different. There was fear and dread and something else. Hemingway had named it. *Nada.* "Some lived in it and never felt it but he [Hemingway's Spanish waiter] knew it was all *nada y pues nada y nada y pues nada y nada.*" Hail nothing. All the lives, all the money, all the destruction. And all for nothing. Hail nothing, the nothing that would always be. A sleeping car is a fine place for not sleeping. "After all," Hemingway's waiter said to himself as he hunted for a bodega, open all night, to take the place of the clean, well-lighted cafe which insisted on closing up, "it is probably only insomnia. Many must have it."

THE THIRD WORLD / *To Make a Prairie*

My third world is still in the making. It is a world of marvel, of scientific miracles. It still has its moments of glory. When America put a man on the moon, I wanted to live forever in order to see what those mighty machines and mighty men of science would discover as they started gadding about the universe. "One giant leap for mankind." Except for one thing. Something science could not provide. We are all insomniacs. And worse than insomnia is nada. Old people complain of loneliness. Young ones say, "I can't find myself. I just can't, you know, get my head together, you know. What's the use of it all, you know?'' Hail nothing. Such feelings set many to rummaging about in old religions or new cults. But perhaps for the old the best that could be hoped was a clean, well-lighted place that stayed open all night and an always available game of bingo. And for the young a commune, a gang, a new monasticism, a gulping materialism.

The earth too suffered. Polluted air, polluted water, whole species of animals disappearing forever. In their place emptiness. Ioway was gone, Iowa going, the black earth disappearing under concrete, a whole farm swallowed by every cloverleaf on a new four-lane highway.

Now every bit of the prairie that had seemed so endless to Trinket, Rover, and three children in the back seat of a surrey was something to cherish. Old bits of surviving prairie were hunted out, restored, and new ones made.

Perhaps it was recoverable after all—that feeling I had had in childhood that I, the meadow, the woodlands, were all one. But from now on, I knew, we would have to make our own prairie.

Prairie

To make a prairie it
 takes a clover and one bee,
One clover and a bee
And revery.
The revery alone will do
If bees are few.

EMILY DICKINSON

Insomnia must give way to revery. But we must understand Emily. The revery alone will do only if it restores what I had thought as a child that the prairie was: a fair meadow of peace inside and outside ourselves. To have peace within oneself—that would be to be grown up. To have it outside ourselves—there may be a chance if the world can learn the meaning of revery of Emily's sort. If it can, the revery alone will do. But the revery we must have.

Photo by Paul A. Christiansen

"Old bits of surviving prairie were hunted out, restored, and new ones made."

RECONSTRUCTED PRAIRIE NEAR CORNELL COLLEGE CAMPUS AT MOUNT VERNON.